The Simon & Schuster
Listener's Guides to Music

CLASSICAL MUSIC: Orchestral

by Alan Rich
with the assistance of Daniel Schillaci

D1113070

A FIRESIDE BOOK
PUBLISHED BY SIMON AND SCHUSTER

A Quarto Book

Copyright © 1980 by Quarto Marketing, Ltd. and Alan Rich

A Fireside Book
Published by Simon and Schuster
A Division of the Gulf & Western Corporation
Simon & Schuster Building
Rockefeller Center
1230 Avenue of Americas
New York, New York 10020

FIRESIDE and Colophon are trademarks of Simon
& Schuster.

SIMON AND SCHUSTER and Colophon are trademarks of
Simon & Schuster.

1   2   3   4   5   6   7   8   9   10

———————————————◄ ♦ ►———————————————

The *Listener's Guide* series was conceived and
edited by John Smallwood
Designed by Tricia Grantz

Production: Millie Falcaro
Picture Research: Michelle Flaum

Produced and prepared by Quarto Marketing, Ltd.

Manufactured in the United States of America
Printed and bound by The Maple-Vail Manufacturing Group

———————————————◄ ♦ ►———————————————

Library of Congress Cataloging in Publication Data
Rich, Alan.
The Simon & Schuster listener's guide
to Classical music.
(A Fireside book)
Includes discographies.
1.   Classical music—Analysis, appreciation.
I.   Title.
MT125.R5   785   80–5076
ISBN 0–671–25440–5
ISBN 0–671–25441–3 (pbk.)

CONTENTS

Daniel Schillaci was of measureless assistance in preparing this first in a series of Listener's Guides *that, with a little bit o' luck, could run forever. In a book such as this, where every omission of music worth the hearing brought its own kind of heartbreak, it was of vital importance to have someone, of free spirit and some belligerence, challenge every decision, argue every word, and furnish some valuable insights and quite a lot of writing. It helped that Danny's tastes in music are not always my own; it means that every work herein discussed is the result of some kind of argument, usually hard-won, all of them contributing energy to the final product.*

A.R.

INTRODUCTION

The aim of this slim volume, and of its companion volumes in this series of *Listener's Guides*, is to answer questions for somebody who already enjoys music, and would like to enjoy it more. Let's say you've just been to a concert, or heard a record—a Mozart symphony, for the sake of argument. You find yourself saying, Who is this Mozart, and what is it about his music that makes my heart beat a little faster? What else did he write besides the symphony I've just heard? Who were the other composers of his time whose music I might also like? And, finally, what are the good recordings of music by Mozart and his contemporaries? Who says they're good, and why?

The aim of this book is to go a little farther than a simple chronology of great composers: to serve, quite literally, as a listeners guide, a nontechnical and highly personal guide to the way music can be listened to. That's tricky, of course; the key word here is personal. A work of art, someone wrote, is like a two-sided mirror. One side reflects the creator of that work—the composer of the symphony, the painter of the picture. The other side reflects the person who is being reached by that art—the listener to the symphony, the observer of the painting.

Nobody can tell anyone else exactly what that other person should hear in a piece of music, beyond some information about the bare bones of that composer's personal musical style. All any writer can do is to approach a reader-listener with something like this: "Here is a piece of music that I like; here are some of the basic facts about this piece; this is why I like it. You are free to like it or dislike it—after you've heard it."

This particular book will be about music for orchestra—symphonic music as it is sometimes called, although that term is somewhat restricting. The book is a history of the overture, the suite, the concerto, the symphony, the tone poem—all the kinds of music that composers have written for orchestra since the first orchestra was formed some three centuries ago. It is written for the listener who already has some vague notion of what those words—overture, symphony, and so forth—mean, and wants to go on from there.

The plan of the book is simplicity itself; history guides the pen. The book is separated into five historical periods, starting with the first truly orchestral music, around 1680, and ending with a brief and cautious look at the electronic music of tomorrow that—it is feared in some circles—could replace symphony orchestras completely. Each section will begin with a few introductory pages that will make some generalizations about the musical style of the period. That will be followed by studies of the major composers of that period, including a list of selected compositions representative of their stylistic evolution and also of the myriad pleasures their music affords. Each selected composition is accompanied by a selected recording, along with some highly personal words as to why that particular recording was selected.

These selected lists, please bear in mind, have been compiled with care, and with enormous sadness. It is indeed sad to have to restrict a list of Mozart's piano concertos to a mere five, when knowing all the while of at least ten others that cannot under any circumstances be lived without. It is just as sad to restrict the choice of a favorite recording of Schubert's "Great" C-major Symphony to one or two, when the catalogues list no fewer than a dozen valid ways to unravel this knotty score.

Bear in mind, then, that the imperfections of this kind of a selective list are at least as important as the assumed excellences. This book must, therefore, serve as a jumping-off point for further explorations. There are other composers in the firmament of orchestral masters than the few stars singled out here. A brief list of supplementary listening is appended at the end of each chapter, but that list in itself is merely a beginning.

What are the criteria for record selection? This is, again, a highly personal matter, for the reasons suggested earlier. There are, to be sure, certain standards for evaluating a performance. Given the size of the orchestra that Bach was writing for, it is not very likely that an orchestra of proper size for Tchaikovsky will come very close to Bach's own musical notions. Beware, though: a great deal of sloppy, or just plain dull, musical performance hides behind a smokescreen of "authenticity," as if a rendition of a Bach concerto using all the "right" instruments from Bach's own time deserves thereby a pipeline to heaven. Nonsense. A dull performance of Bach on an authentic 18th-century harpsichord communicates far less than an intelligent, loving, and elegantly controlled performance on a modern grand piano, however anachronistic. We have to remember that the listening audience in the 1980s cannot hear music the way Bach's intimate circle did; too much has happened in and to music between Bach's death in 1750 and our own time.

Every attempt has been made to include in the selected lists only recordings with a fair chance of remaining in circulation (barring, of course, an outbreak of mass insanity in the record industry). At the same time, attention is given to certain great performances of the past, which may have been reissued on LP and which are decidedly worth the effort to track down. These may be monaural recordings rather than the latest digitalized stereo; they may, indeed, date back to the days of records revolving at 78 revolutions per minute. But some great recorded performances, like all great music, are—or ought to be—eternal.

NOTE TO READERS IN BRITAIN
In some cases, the US labels given in the selected recordings are not the same in Britain. Usually, United States' *London* label, for example, is *Decca* in Britain, *Columbia* is *CBS*, and *Angel* is *HMV*. Where changes occur, the British label is given second in the listing. Readers are advised to consult a current *Gramophone Classical Catalogue* if they have difficulty in finding a recording.

The Baroque

The lights in the concert hall are dimmed as the conductor arrives at the podium—greeted, with any luck, by warm applause from the audience and a polite response from the orchestra. That orchestra is an assemblage of anywhere from thirty to a hundred musicians, each a master of one of a wide variety of instruments. These musicians are seated on stage according to a plan that has developed, with some flexibility, over a century or more. So has the plan of the orchestra itself, the proportion of one kind of instrument to another. There are more stringed instruments than woodwinds, brass, or percussion. There are more violins, among the strings, than there are violas, cellos, or double basses.

The exact size of the orchestra can vary somewhat, especially in the number of strings, according to the orchestra's budget and the size of the hall. The proportions, however—more strings than winds, for example—exist simply because, over the time the symphony orchestra has flourished as a musical force, composers have found that these proportions work. They have found that an ensemble of strings, winds, brass, and percussion, give or take additions or subtractions within a finite range, can produce a wide variety of sounds. And they have been encouraged by the fact that audiences at orchestral concerts take pleasure in these sounds, and are emotionally reached by the masterpieces that use the sounds well.

In fact, it can be said that of all the different kinds of music that make up what we loosely refer to as "serious" or "classical" (meaning, if any meaning there be, music of deliberate design intended to be listened to as an end in itself, as opposed to music to be danced or marched to, eaten or drunk to, or otherwise participated in by its hearers), symphonic music has reached the widest audience and enjoys the greatest popularity. There are many reasons for this, social and economic as well as artistic. The only reason with which this book is concerned, however, is the most basic: that out of the resources of the symphony orchestra has come a vast repertoire of great music.

In one sense, the orchestra occupies a surprisingly small proportion of the total history of music. Musical historians generally begin their serious work on music from around 1000 AD—not because there hadn't been music before that time, but because that was the time of the first decipherable system for writing down music. Out of this period of roughly a millennium, the orchestra only makes its appearance for the last 250 of those years. Considering Johann Sebastian Bach (1685–1750) as the first great composer of orchestral music, we can see that Bach was a latecomer in the overall historical spectrum. There existed already a long tradition that included music for church observance, vocal music for secular use, music for solo instruments and small ensembles, and music created for the theater or opera.

The notion of creating music for a group of assorted musical instruments did not occur to any one composer in one single burst of inspiration. There have been musical instruments as long as there has been music, and we have the evidence of scholarly treatises, unscholarly diaries, and paintings to prove the existence of great noisy instrumental ensembles in ancient times.

How, then, can we establish a starting date for the orchestra, as we know it today? In this way: the orchestra differs from a random assortment of instruments in that the composer sets down, in what is known as a score, specific parts of his composition to be played by specific instruments. What he is doing, in mandating the exact tone color in his composition, was then, and is now, known as orchestration. And it wasn't until the end of the 17th century, in Italy, that orchestration became an important part of instrumental music.

It happened then, and there, for two basic reasons. One was that Italy in the late 17th century was an operatic madhouse from one end of the country to the other. Opera, the setting of a drama to music in such a way as to enhance the emotion of the drama, was more or less invented in Florence around 1600. In 1637 the first public opera house opened in Venice, to be followed by others in Rome, Naples, and elsewhere. With the exception of a few noble works of Alessandro Scarlatti and one or two others, however, Italian opera by the late 17th century was a rather trashy affair, mostly designed to show off the exquisite tastelessness of great vocal virtuosos. Artificial as most of these works were, they had the one unmistakably Italian quality: great melodic outpouring.

At about the height of the Italian opera craze, in the Lombard town of Cremona, a group of instrument makers—among them several members of the Amati family, and a younger disciple named Antonio Stradivari—made certain radical improvements in the design of stringed instruments. These changes imparted a singing tone of sweetness hitherto unheard-of from a mere instrument and, with a changed design, allowed for astounding feats of virtuosity. The result was a new craze: music for violin, viola, and cello that could rival in poignancy and agility the work of the most adored opera singers.

By 1700, in the hands of such composers as Arcangelo Corelli (1653–1713), Giuseppe Torelli (1658–1709), and Tommaso Albinoni (1671–1750), a repertoire of phenomenal popularity had taken shape in the north of Italy that rivaled the fame of opera. Corelli and his compatriots, indeed, had invented a brilliant solo style for the newly improved stringed instruments, and had also developed a writing style for these instruments in ensemble, with the layout of parts exactly specified to create the composer's own prescription for tone color. The orchestra, in other words, was born.

Orchestras developed at the palaces of many major Italian cities; the solo virtuosos—Corelli himself, for one—were in such demand that noblemen from city to city tried to outbid one another for a particular player's services. To the north, German dukes and princes imported whole Italian ensembles to become resident at one or another palace, to play for noble assemblages, and to teach their art to noble youngsters. The young Johann Sebastian Bach, serving as court musician at the small principality of Anhalt-Cöthen, heard the new Italian music and was deeply impressed. Both as a tribute and as a means of studying this music, Bach transcribed a number of these orchestral works into new versions for solo harpsichord or organ. Then he boldly tried his own hand at composition in this style, expanding the scope to include virtuoso performers on instruments other than strings. The result was the set of six masterful "Brandenburg" Concertos, which include solos for oboe, horns, trumpet, flute, and harpsichord.

The Italians called this new music the concerto; the exact meaning—"to vie with" or "to strive against"—suggests how close to the dramatic world of opera these composers saw themselves. In the typical Italian concerto, there are either three or four separate movements, alternating fast-slow-fast or slow-fast-slow-fast. Within each movement there are further contrasts: a small group of instruments, three or four, alternating with the more massive sound of the full orchestra, or a solo instrument against the full orchestra—the triumph of virtue over force, or some such.

The public concert hall—the place where, for the price of entry, any member of the public might enjoy a musical performance—came into being only late in the 18th century. Bach himself composed for orchestras while in the employ of several German noblemen, but not once in his lifetime did he enjoy what we would think of as a public performance of his orchestral music, before a paying, applauding audience. Actually, it was Bach's youngest son, Johann Christian, who opened one of the world's first public concert halls where tickets were sold for the latest symphonies and concertos of the day. That was in London in the 1770s; by 1800, most major European cities were witnessing their first orchestra-going audiences.

The history of symphonic music is inextricably tied to the history of the musical consumer. This phenomenon, in turn, arose as part of an even greater social upheaval, whose symptoms became evident on opposite sides of the world: overthrow of the French monarchy by the popular revolution of 1789 and, simultaneously, the overthrow of British rule by the American colonies. Much that we now take for granted as public property was, until that fateful time, cordoned off for the exclusive use of a finite aristocracy. And so it was with music.

Antonio Vivaldi

b Venice (date uncertain, sometime between 1669 and 1678); *d* Vienna, July 26, 1741. Principal output includes: concertos (possibly as many as 800) for string orchestra with supporting harpsichord and for solo instruments or multiple soloists with orchestra. Also: operas (possibly as many as forty); church music (oratorios, cantatas, masses, vesper services); and secular vocal music.

A 1713 visitor's guide to Venice mentions among the city's musical amenities the playing of its solo musicians. "Among the best," the book states, "are Gian-Battista Vivaldi and his son, priest." That is almost the first notation we have about the "son, priest," who was to become the most popular composer of his own time, to vanish from popularity for two centuries, and then to return to sweep the charts once again in our own time.

Vivaldi, ordained in 1703 and popularly known as the "Red Priest" for reasons assumed to be tonsorial, found his early musical fulfillment within his priestly duties. Assigned to the Conservatory at the church-controlled Ospedale della Pietà, one of four Venetian institutions housing illegitimate or orphaned girls, Vivaldi soon discovered a remarkably high percentage of musical talent among his charges. From 1704 to 1740 his major job was to instruct the girls in violin, direct the orchestra, and most important, compose music for that ensemble in what became an endless stream.

The church fathers seemed to approve of Vivaldi's ministrations, since the annals of the Ospedale indicate that the resident maestro was granted frequent leaves of absence to spread his own fame into other European capitals. Mention exists in several German cities and in Paris of Vivaldi concerts, enthusiastically attended. The new violin technique pioneered by Corelli was catching on, and apparently Vivaldi was one of its most eloquent proponents. It was on one of those journeys that Vivaldi, either in person or through his music, came to the attention of Johann Sebastian Bach, then serving at the ducal court of Anhalt-Cöthen. Bach fell upon the music, and paid it tribute by arranging it and passing it off as his own—a common and condoned practice at the time.

Soon, however, Vivaldi's public career began to undermine his priestly duties, and when, around 1740, some official happened to note that Vivaldi had not said mass in 25 years, fur flew. Vivaldi left the church, spent a few months composing opera, and died a year later.

Pick up any but the most scholarly book on music published before 1950, and you will most likely find that if the name Vivaldi appears at all, it will probably figure simply because J. S. Bach arranged some of his music to suit his own purposes. Pick up the latest long-playing record catalogue, however, and you'll find that literally hundreds of works by the "Red Priest" are listed, many in recordings many times duplicated.

The sudden rediscovery of Vivaldi shortly after the Second World War has many explanations. It seems to have been triggered by the revival of one specific work, a set of four three-movement concertos for solo violin and string orchestra, to which Vivaldi had appended a set of his own poems describing *The Four Seasons* (a popular conceit for painters of the time as well as poets and composers). Not only was there the poetry to go with the concertos; there was also Vivaldi's own fanciful use of both soloist and orchestra to imitate the sound of birds, of buzzing insects, of thunder, of ice cracking on a pond. First published among a set of 12 concertos in 1725 but virtually unknown after Vivaldi's death until 1939, and first recorded in 1948 (in a hideously romanticized reorchestration by one

Bernardino Molinari), the music burst on a world that seemed urgently in need of exactly that kind of surprise and delight. (More "authentic" performances on records, needless to say, were not long in arriving.) Perhaps it was simply that the world had heard too much heavily orchestrated romantic music; perhaps it was that the clean, crisp sounds of the Baroque orchestra were a dandy test for all the hi-fidelity equipment that was coming on the market in 1948 in the wake of the invention of the LP. In any case, Vivaldi took off like a rocket, and shows no sign of coming down.

That Vivaldi was incredibly prolific—upwards of 600 concertos for strings alone have been credited to his name so far, with new caches periodically uncovered—may be explained by his duties as teacher of music and orchestra leader at a Venetian seminary, where the prime pedagogical device consisted of an endless stream of new music to play. A wag's statement—that Vivaldi actually composed the same concerto 600 times—is at least partially unfair, as *The Four Seasons* and a fair number of other works, in which a volatile expressive passion is almost always at hand, amply prove. The vast majority of the teaching pieces do seem to have a deadly predictability. Yet there is, in listening carefully to Vivaldi, an element a little like living under a volcano. There is a fine madness in his work, and eruptions—sudden shifts of sonority, of harmony, of a tune that begins blandly and suddenly darts into the middle of next week—often come when you least expect them. The ultimate disservice to Vivaldi is, unfortunately, still to be observed at certain social gatherings: a record changer loaded with half a dozen collections of Vivaldi concertos, made to serve under cocktail conversation as a faintly audible wallpaper. No composer, no matter how strong his predilection for sanitary symmetry, deserves this.

SELECTED RECORDINGS

The Four Seasons (Concertos Nos. 1–4 from Opus 8)
–Karl Münchinger and the Stuttgart Chamber Orchestra (London)

L'Estro armonico (Twelve Concertos, Opus 3)
   –Neville Marriner and the Academy of St. Martin-in-the-Fields (Argo)
Four Concertos for Solo Winds and Orchestra
   –Max Goberman and the New York Sinfonietta (Columbia-Odyssey)
Concertos for Diverse Instruments
   –Leonard Bernstein and the New York Philharmonic (Columbia)

Out of the dozens of recordings of *The Four Seasons* issued over the years, the clear, simple logic of Münchinger's performance continues to glow. (Careful, though, to insist on the version listed above; there is an earlier Münchinger performance not nearly as good.) You can, if you wish, acquire performances by koto ensembles, a transcription for flute and strings, an academically interesting but still rather dull version using instruments and bows of Vivaldi's own time, and performances by very large and very small orchestras. They merely cast all the more favorable light on the performance chosen.

The twelve concertos of *L'Estro armonico* (possibly translatable as "The Harmonic Sexual Frenzy") are all superior examples of Vivaldi's string writing. The D-minor Concerto comes closest to exemplifying the strange title; its fast movements are almost brutally passionate, while the ethereal slow movement can break your heart. The set also includes the B-minor Concerto with four solo violins; Bach arranged this same music as a concerto for four solo harpsichords: in either version, another extremely dark, passionate piece. Marriner's little English ensemble plays with an ideal blend of authenticity and emotion.

The two collections of concertos for various solo instruments contain enchanting music, and offer an interesting contrast between two altogether valid ways of performing this music: the small-scale elegance of the pickup group under the late, beloved Goberman and Bernstein's extroverted style with a larger orchestra. That both styles work speaks volumes about the universality of Vivaldi.

Johann Sebastian Bach

b Eisenach, Germany, March 21, 1685; *d* Leipzig, July 28, 1750. Principal output includes: innumerable concertos for one, two, three, or four violins, harpsichords, or assorted instruments; six concerti grossi (known as the "Brandenburg" Concertos) for variously constituted solo groups with strings; four suites (or "overtures") for orchestra; sacred and secular choral music (cantatas, passions, masses, motets, and songs); keyboard compositions in vast variety; speculative works in open score (*A Musical Offering, The Art of the Fugue*); sonatas; suites; and partitas for various solo instruments alone or with harpsichord.

At the time of his death in Leipzig at the age of 65, Johann Sebastian Bach was known primarily as one of the supreme masters of the organ. As a composer, he had never been either fashionable or famous. Few of his contemporaries had any inkling that he was any more than another solid, reliable craftsman, member of a family that had produced many such (and was, through Johann Sebastian, to produce many more). But, in succeeding generations, many came to regard him as the greatest musician of all.

Bach was never an innovator; in his own musical tastes he was, if anything, reactionary. His elaborate contrapuntal style harked back in some ways to the Renaissance a century and more before; to his contemporaries this style was already regarded as intractable. His own sons, many of whom became composers more famous in their own time than their father in his, showed little inclination to follow their father's style. They were already of another era.

Yet the culminating figures of that later, classic era, Haydn and Mozart, were to return to Bach's music, and draw inspiration therefrom, late in their own lives.

This happened largely through the influence of a Viennese dilettante, Baron van Swieten, who himself had unearthed many of Bach's forgotten scores and had them performed at his own musicales—forty years after Bach's death.

Bach never attained the worldly success of his contemporaries, Vivaldi, Handel, and Telemann, nor did he seek it. Yet he did have a consuming curiosity about international musical styles. His orchestral music was composed for the most part early in his career (1717–23), when, as Kapellmeister and director of chamber music for Prince Leopold of Anhalt at Cöthen, he had an orchestra of eighteen musicians to compose for and direct. Visiting Italian musicians brought the music of Vivaldi and other Italians to this court, and Bach was fascinated by the new music from the south. During this time he created a great many concertos for solo or multiple instruments with string orchestra supported by harpsichord. Vivaldi's music had a strong influence on these works; indeed, Bach adapted many of Vivaldi's works literally for his own use as conductor and organist.

Yet these concertos of Bach were far from slavish imitations of Italian models. His own North German intellect was also engaged, and some of the most brilliant movements are worked out as intricate multiple fugues. There is also in these works a tense, dramatic quality that comes about largely from a free, sometimes quite startling use of dissonance. Listen, for example, to the slow movement of the first in the marvelous set of six "Brandenburg" Concertos from the Anhalt-Cöthen years—hardly the writing of a careful conservative!

Bach's last years were spent at Leipzig, where his principal task was the creation of service music for two large Lutheran congregations. At a Collegium Musicum at the University of Leipzig during that time, however, Bach could again indulge his love of instrumental writing. For Leipzig he rewrote many of his former concertos for violin or wind instruments into totally new works for solo or multiple harpsichords. Comparisons between older and newer versions are fascinating; the working of one of the greatest minds in music is made clear for all to study and admire.

SELECTED RECORDINGS

Six "Brandenburg" Concertos
–Various soloists with Paul Baumgartner and the
Lucerne Festival Strings (Deutsche Grammophon)
–Otto Klemperer and the Philharmonia Orchestra
(Angel)

Three-Harpsichord Concerto in D Minor; Four-Harpsichord Concerto in A minor
–Various soloists with Raymond Leppard and the
English Chamber Orchestra (Philips)

Three-Harpsichord Concertos in C major and D minor
–Rudolf Serkin, Mieczyslaw Horszowski, and Ruth
Laredo, pianists, with Alexander Schneider and the
Marlboro Festival Orchestra (Columbia)

Violin-Oboe Concerto in C minor; Two-Violin Concerto in D minor; Two-Harpsichord Concerto in C minor
–Various soloists with Karl Richter and the
Munich Bach Orchestra (Deutsche Grammophon)

Violin Concertos No. 1 in A minor and No. 2 in E major
–Nathan Milstein and a chamber orchestra (Angel)

Four Suites for Orchestra
–Karl Münchinger and the Stuttgart Chamber
Orchestra (London)
–Nicolaus Harnoncourt and the Concentus
Musicus (Telefunken)

Much richness, here, and much variety in both music
and performance. The clean, neatly phrased Baumgartner recording of the "Brandenburgs" is an excellent compromise between scholarly "authenticity" and
contemporary taste, while Klemperer's more grandiose
performance will please those who want a plummier
approach. At least Klemperer enlarges the scope of the
music in reasonably exact proportions. The three- and
four-harpsichord pieces are marvelous clatter; the one
for four harpsichords is an arrangement by Bach (free
enough to be considered a paraphrase) of Vivaldi's
Concerto for Four Violins (from his *L'Estro armonico*, see
page 8); the keyboard version was also used in the Jean
Cocteau movie *Les Enfants Terribles*. The piano version

of the three-harpsichord version is included to show how marvelous and caring musicians, even using anachronistic instruments, can bring old music to life.

The slow movements of the violin-oboe and two-violin concertos are all anyone needs to demonstrate the poignancy and warmth of Bach's melodic style; both works, in fact, stand high among all of Bach's concertos. (The two-violin concerto is the music for George Balanchine's fabulous ballet *Concerto Barocco*.) And another musician usually associated with the more overtly romantic repertoire, Nathan Milstein, proves his versatility in these loving, sensitive performances of the two powerful works for violin and orchestra.

The Four Suites for Orchestra (also sometimes called *Overtures*) also date from Bach's early years, although it is likely that he revised them extensively later on. They are similar in layout to many of his solo keyboard works—the Partitas and the French Suites—in consisting of an extended festive overture followed by a series of dance-like movements and contrasting "airs." The well-known "Air on the G String," beloved by violinists as an encore tidbit, is the slow movement from the Third Suite.

The Münchinger and Harnoncourt performances are at the opposite ends of the range of what we define today as "authentic" Baroque performance: the former, a glowing treatment, using the proper-sized orchestra but with modern instruments eloquently played; the latter, an absolutely "correct" version using instruments of Bach's own time played in what scholars discern as a Bachian style—interesting as a document but lifeless as music. A question for the scholars: if music was ever meant to be this dull, how come the art has survived so long?

Georg Friedrich Handel

(later anglicized to George Frideric). *b* Halle, Germany, February 23, 1685; *d* London, April 14, 1759. Principal output includes: orchestral music (concertos, suites of dances, twelve concerti grossi, music for royal occasions); operas in Italian and

English; oratorios and other dramatic religious music in German, Italian, and English; chamber music; and works for keyboard solo.

Johann Sebastian Bach spent his life in isolation, seldom if ever known more than a mile or two from his places of employment—first the various small courts of Germany and later the provincial city of Leipzig. The great Italian masters of the Baroque orchestra similarly enjoyed little fame abroad, and then only among their particular patron and the guests at his musical evenings. Before anything else is said for or against George Frideric Handel, therefore, he must be recognized as the first composer in the history of music to become a celebrity in the eyes of a vast, adoring public.

Clumsy in appearance, ill-tempered, barely able to speak the language of the London where he spent most of his life, Handel at least managed his musical career with great shrewdness. He had consecrated his life to music at an early age, and soon after realized that his native Saxony was too small, artistically speaking, for his ambitions. He toured Italy, carefully noting the kinds of music in its various cities that most pleased the crowds. He returned to Germany, the equal of any Italian in writing Italian opera and Italian orchestral music. He then sniffed the air, discovering that of all countries England had the greatest hunger for Italian music. In 1710, age 25, Handel settled in London, and seldom budged from there.

For his English audiences the German Handel wrote the best Italian operas of any composer of the day. When, around 1740, the public taste for this music waned, he became a composer of oratorio (like opera, derived from Italian models), which, though unstaged, he made even more dramatic and grandiose than opera. The best known of these, *Messiah*, is, despite its musical splendor, actually the least dramatic. Compare to this, for example, the incredible description of the Crossing of the Red Sea, with two choruses and orchestras thundering out the glory of God, in *Israel in*

Egypt. Now imagine this golden noise resounding down the nave of a huge British cathedral, and you'll understand why Handel was the hero of his day.

From Italy, too, Handel acquired skill as an orchestral composer. His most famous work is the so-called *Water Music,* three suites of Baroque airs and dances that may or may not have been played on royal barges in the Thames on a summer night in 1717, and that may or may not have served to heal a rift between Handel and his royal patron (and fellow Saxon) George I. The marvelous set of twelve concerti grossi are noble and rather daring paraphrases on the models Handel had heard in Italy, drawing much drama from the interplay of small and large groups of players.

All of Handel's music, like that of Mozart years hence, should be thought of as the work of a composer with a passion for drama and for powerful dramatic effects. Much of his best instrumental music—the organ concertos, for example—were interpolated into oratorio performances, and share the oratorio's tendency for massive sounds. Polite performances of these concertos or of the great bit of noise (for brass bands and winds) written in 1749 for a royal fireworks display, miss the point as badly as a polite performance of, say, the Hallelujah Chorus from *Messiah.*

Unlike Bach or the Italian Baroque masters, Handel never suffered an eclipse. His music has suffered other forms of mistreatment, however, particularly in his adopted England. The very popularity of his music, especially the oratorios, has given rise to a Handelian style consisting mostly of bellowing. Much of his orchestral music, reorchestrated by later performers for massive, contemporary orchestral forces, has been made to bellow, too. That is hardly necessary; the trick in performing Handel is to realize that the music, as originally written, was the lustiest stuff of its day. An imaginative performer can preserve that quality today without violating the music itself.

SELECTED RECORDINGS

Concerti Grossi, Opus 6
–Neville Marriner and the Academy of St. Martin-in-the-Fields (London)

Concertos for Organ and Strings
   –E. Power Biggs, soloist, with Sir Adrian Boult and
   the London Philharmonic Orchestra (Columbia)
   –Simon Preston, soloist, with Yehudi Menuhin and
   the Bath Festivals Orchestra (Angel)
Concertos for Two Wind Choirs and Strings
   –Raymond Leppard and the English Chamber
   Orchestra (Philips)
Water Music
   –Pierre Boulez and the New York Philharmonic
   (Columbia)

The above selection should provide a fair overview of
both Handel's own range of composition and of the
range possible among contemporary performances that
can still fall short of violating the proportions of the
music. Marriner's impeccable taste, and the skill of his
small London ensemble, make him an ideal Handel interpreter; it would be hard to imagine adherents of any
style of performance objecting to his work. The deep
seriousness, the melodic nobility (obviously Italian-
inspired) of the concerti grossi bring out special qualities in Marriner's work.

As for the organ concertos, Biggs and Boult belong
to a somewhat older school of Handelians. They are
faithful to the proportions of the music, but everything is slightly enlarged, slightly lustier than in, say,
the elegant (and equally beautiful) Preston-Menuhin
performance.

The works for double wind-choir are among the
most gorgeous examples extant of what used to be
called the "glorious Handelian racket." One or two
movements are taken from *Water Music* and other
sources, proving that Handel himself was not above
reorchestrating his own music. Leppard's ardent love
of early music takes the form at times of a great deal
of freedom in the matter of interpretation and im-
provisation; while some scholars tend to sniff at the
practice, the extreme beauty of most of his work
should be all that matters.

The Boulez *Water Music* may not be the most Handelian interpretation either (there are fine Menuhin
and Marriner performances of quieter mien), yet the
individuality and unfailing interest in Boulez's own
sharply defined rhythms and the stunning detail in the

work of his orchestra make his performance worth sampling.

One final note: while Handel's music did suffer at the hands of arrangers, especially in the last century, some reorchestrations were at least conceived as acts of love, and are worth hearing. Among them are Sir Thomas Beecham's suite of excerpts from the opera *The Faithful Shepherd* and Sir Hamilton Harty's splendidly noisy if abbreviated versions of *Water Music* and *Music for the Royal Fireworks*. All these have survived transfer to LP, and are worth hunting down—in monaural versions, ancient of course, conducted by the respective perpetrators.

SUPPLEMENTARY COMPOSERS

Henry Purcell (c 1659–1695)
Ballet Suites from *Abdelazar, The Gordian Knot Untied, The Married Beau, The Virtuous Wife*
–Fritz Mahler and a chamber orchestra (Vanguard)

Arcangelo Corelli (1653–1713)
Concerti Grossi for String Orchestra, Opus 6
–Neville Marriner and the Academy of St. Martin-in-the Fields (No. 8 of this set is the famous "Christmas" Concerto) (Argo)

Wilhelm Friedemann Bach (1710–1784)
Sinfonia in D minor; Two Minuets
–Nicholas Flagello and the Rome Chamber Orchestra (also includes a concerto by Carl Philipp Emanuel Bach and a work by Georg Philipp Telemann) (Peters)

Georg Philipp Telemann (1681–1767)
Concertos for Oboe d'Amore and Strings
(for Flute, Oboe d'Amore, and Violin and Strings; for Two Violas.)
–Various soloists with Antonio Janigro and I Solisti di Zagreb (Vanguard)
Concertos and Overtures for Trumpets, Oboes, and Strings
–Various soloists with Karl Ristenpart and the Saar Chamber Orchestra (Nonesuch)

"Water Music" (Hamburg's Ebb and Flow); Concerto for Three Violins and Strings
–Paris Collegium Musicum (Nonesuch)

Purcell, the foremost English composer of his time, and arguably the foremost native British composer of *any* time, studied for a while in Italy. His own style, therefore, was influenced by the Italian string writers (among them Corelli), who were, in turn, influenced by the passionate melody of Italian opera. All this came together in Purcell's own music with a musical daring that was his alone. He composed little for orchestra as such; his vocal music, both sacred and secular, gives the best insight into his work. But these suites of dances and airs from various of his dramatic scores (not exactly operas, more like extensive sets of background music and songs for plays of the time) demonstrate the extraordinary freshness of his music.

It is particularly interesting to compare Purcell's music with the serene gravity of Corelli's own string writing. Corelli did not bequeath a large musical output, but this one set of string concertos was vastly influential over later composers (Vivaldi among them), and deeply beautiful in themselves.

Of J. S. Bach's twenty children, many became composers, trained initially, of course, by their father. Most of them were already of a new musical generation, which is described in the next chapter. Wilhelm Friedemann, the eldest, remained closest in style to his father's musical ideals; even so, we can hear a new influence—as in the slow movement of the Sinfonia in D minor—a trend toward the simple, singing melody, symmetrical in its phrasing, that presages a new musical era.

The prolific Telemann was, of all his contemporaries, the most cosmopolitan and the most popular. He traveled widely, assimilated the Italian manner (as Handel had), wrote in the elegant dance-inspired style favored by the French, while reaping honor in his own land with such grand tribute-paying pieces as the set of "Water Music" pieces descriptive of the tides at Hamburg. Like Vivaldi, he composed pieces for all conceivable solo instruments or combinations, and the expanse of his output is only now being discovered.

The Classic Era
Music Goes Public

"It went *magnifique*," wrote the 24-year-old Wolfgang Amadeus Mozart to his father. The young man had just had the thrill of hearing one of his symphonies played by a new and splendid Viennese orchestra: "forty violins, twelve double basses, six bassoons, and all the wind doubled." And from other reports of the time we learn that Mozart's orchestra was only one of many flourishing in Vienna at the time, along with similar grand noise-making ensembles in Prague, Linz, Salzburg, Munich, Mannheim—and across the map to Paris and London.

By the last half of the 18th century, the orchestra in all European cities had begun to challenge the opera in popularity. When the young Mozart came to Vienna in 1780, to seek the fortune he never truly achieved, public orchestral concerts were standard fare in several Viennese halls. Mozart himself was to make his strongest impression on the Viennese public in a series of subscription concerts, in which he hired an orchestra and a hall, sold tickets, and presented himself in concerts of brand-new piano concertos that he had composed for these occasions. Even before that, both Mozart and Haydn had composed major orchestral scores for an established public concert series in Paris. And, while Haydn had spent the greater part of his life as composer for and leader of the private orchestra maintained by the Esterházy family at their palace near the Austria-Hungary border, his final triumph was as visiting composer for a series of public orchestral concerts presented by the impresario J. P. Salomon at a large hall in London.

The fact that music "went public" at the end of the 18th century is not a mere historical sidebar to music itself. A new audience meant, for any composer with the intelligence to think things out, a new set of guidelines in the art of musical communication. To move an orchestra from a prince's private music room to a public hall seating 500 and more presented new challenges and opened new horizons.

Long before the death of J. S. Bach in 1750, a new generation of composers—among them several of Bach's own sons whom he himself had taught—were consciously creating a new kind of music. Rejecting the exquisite intricacy of the late Baroque, with its dark passions often expressed in great, cloudy musical structures, the new composers addressed themselves to a simpler music that might find a wide audience—even suitable, as some contemporary advertisements read, "to be played by young ladies in the home." The essence of this music was a beautiful and shapely melodic line discreetly supported by harmony, but without the complex counterpoint of the Bach style.

We call this whole artistic period "classic," and with good reason. It was the time of excavation, of rediscovery and revaluation of the classic heritage. The elegant symmetry of Greek architecture was re-created in thousands of buildings in Europe and in the New World. The balance and clarity of the classic aesthetic were also emulated in the serene composition of Joshua Reynolds' paintings and the pseudo-sculptural canvases of Jacques Louis David. And in music, too, the first generation of classic composers—Johann and Karl Stamitz (father and son), Giovanni Battista Sammartini, Giovanni Battista Pergolesi, and Bach brothers Carl Philipp Emanuel and Johann Christian—evolved a musical aesthetic that enlisted the sublime logic of classic art to reach an audience with a musical language at once clear and emotionally thrilling.

Nobody set out to invent classic musical form. It seems to have fallen into place as the logical consequence of the new musical language. The most important element in that new language was melody—simple, clear, and so shaped that it clearly defined itself as belonging to a certain key. Most of all, the classic melody was an element in the musical design that a listener could easily remember.

At this point, we must make a short and painless digression into musical aesthetics.

Music exists as an audible way of organizing time. To this process the listener contributes two things: memory and curiosity. The composer satisfies memory by furnishing the listener with memorable materials (usually a melody, but just as easily a sonority, a rhythm, or even, conceivably, a certain length of silence) and by bringing back those materials from time to time to let the listener become oriented and suspect the presence of an orderly process of departure and return. Sometimes the materials are returned verbatim, sometimes they are altered. If they were sufficiently memorable to begin with, the composer tends to trust a listener to recognize them even if they are somewhat altered.

Everything else that happens in a piece of music is directed at satisfying the listener's curiosity. The composer extends his musical design, the aforementioned "orderly process," by departing from his original materials, by introducing new and contrasting material. The contrasts can be one or all of the following: a totally different melody, sonority, or rhythm, a change of key or a change from a harmonic style that clearly defines a key to one that arouses uncertainty. The composer has the responsibility, of course, of making his contrast still relate in some way to his previous material. One does not ordinarily drop an apple pie into the middle of a tossed salad.

The roles of memory and curiosity are not mutually exclusive. The new, contrasting material also prints itself on the hearer's memory, and he follows its course and, possibly, the course of still new contrasting material. Yet, in the clear and logical classic forms we're concerned with here, sooner or later the original material returns. That, in the course of an extended work in the late 18th century, is often a moment of high drama. In the works of Beethoven, a few years later on, the drama was often unbearably intense.

The concept of clear and controlled musical

structures did not come into the art overnight. The need to exert some ordering over the interplay of unity and contrast is part of any notion of design at any time. The Baroque concerto, in the hands of Bach, Handel, and Vivaldi, was a work in several contrasting movements somewhat unified by key and by mood, and within a given movement there was always some sense of statement and departure and return. But the obsession with clarity and balance on the part of the classic composer and the kind of melody he came to work with—elegant, symmetrical, and capable of being recognized even when undergoing some degree of manipulation—led to a new clarity of musical organization that was at once precise and wonderfully logical.

The new formal ideals allowed for unity to be achieved through a variety of means. The simplest forms were built out of an alternation of material basically unchanged: A–B–A, A–B–A–C–A . . . , or any number of possible permutations. Sometimes a single idea was used, subjected by the composer to artful variations that served to explore the many possibilities in an innocent-sounding but pregnant tune. The most complex of the classic forms, often known as sonata form, can be a marvelously intricate ordering of many levels of contrast.

In the "typical" sonata-form movement, a theme is stated and is followed by a passage whose purpose is to move into another key. In that new key a contrasting theme is stated, whereupon the first major section of the movement—the "exposition"—is brought to a close. In the ensuing section, called the "development," material already heard may be reheard in new ways—fragments of the themes, for example, played off against one another. In this section, too, there are many changes of key, creating a sense of harmonic insecurity. This, then, leads, often after a great deal of dramatic tension, to a "recapitulation," in which the material from the exposition is restated, but this time without change of key.

This manner of arrangement allows for several kinds of contrast. In the exposition there is contrast between first theme and second theme, first key area and second. The development subjects the themes themselves to new treatment, and also contrasts with the exposition by encompassing many changes of key instead of just two. And the recapitulation contrasts with the development by its greater stability, while providing the sense of unity, of rounding-off, by returning to the material heard at the outset.

But the real beauty of this logical, clear form is the infinite variety with which it can be used. Everything you've read in the last three paragraphs is the basic textbook description of classic form. But the most important thing is that the great composers of the period, and on into the 19th century, for that matter, found infinite ways to respect the spirit of the forms while varying the letter by thousands of devices. Thus, after the teacher has filled his blackboard with diagrams of classic form, if he tries to find music among the masterpieces of the time to illustrate his diagrams note-for-note, he will be out of luck.

Haydn, in his long and productive lifetime, created over 100 symphonies (plus a comparable number of chamber and solo works) that followed the basic outlines of the classic forms; yet, in every one of these works there is a new way of solving one of the problems these forms present, and Haydn's solutions are what give drama to his works and made him the most popular composer of his day. Mozart, the most natural genius the world has known, started writing symphonies at the age of 9, at first merely imitating symphonies he had heard in his native Salzburg. Within a very few years, however, he, too, had invented his own formal solutions, producing, usually for himself to perform, piano concertos that expanded even further the possibilities of formal creation, while borrowing heavily from the devices of opera.

It is in their ability to conquer the aesthetic of an era obsessed with structure and symmetry, to maintain their own profoundly original voices, that Haydn and Mozart tower over the works of their hundreds of bustling contemporaries. Music, in its early years of public life, was enormously popular throughout the civilized world, and there was work for all. Much has survived from the pens of such excellent composers as Boccherini, Cimarosa, Salieri, and others who were revered in Vienna while Mozart went hungry. Genius doesn't always win out in its own time, but history usually sets things right.

Franz Joseph Haydn

b Rohrau, Lower Austria, March 31, 1732; *d* Vienna, May 31, 1809. Principal output includes: orchestral music (104 authenticated symphonies, several others probably authentic; concertos for violin, cello, trumpet, horn, and keyboard; and incidental music—serenades, nocturnes, and divertimentos); chamber music (including nearly eighty string quartets; nearly fifty trios for piano, violin, and cello; nearly 100 trios for strings alone; and countless works for other combinations); and piano sonatas. Also: operas (including works for marionette players); religious music (including fourteen masses); oratorios; songs; and cantatas.

Few composers in history were granted the ideal creative conditions under which Haydn spent most of his life. Few composers, given so great a benefice, proved themselves more worthy than Haydn. A modest Croatian organist and part-time composer when, at 29, he was hired as Kapellmeister to Prince Anton Esterházy at the family's estate at Eisenstadt in eastern Austria, Haydn was to retire from that service thirty years later, revered and sought after throughout Europe.

After Prince Anton died in 1762, his brother, Nikolaus, acceded to the title. The arts have known no more enlightened patron. To the Esterházy palace Nikolaus brought the finest performers money could buy, and placed this fabulously talented orchestra at Haydn's disposal with the sole condition that Haydn be as daring as his artistic conscience might allow. The results were extraordinary; in Haydn's hands the great instrumental forms of the classic era—most of all the string quartet, the trio for piano, violin, and cello, and the symphony—were forged into a state of sublime expressiveness.

To say that no two of Haydn's symphonies are at all like one another is to stretch a point only slightly. Nearly 80 of his 104 symphonies were composed for the Esterházy orchestra, and together they represent a fantastic laboratory for the exploration of the expressive potential within the classic orchestra and the classic aesthetic. The first three symphonies for Esterházy form a descriptive trilogy: *Morning, Noon,* and *Evening,* in which the orchestra not only imitates the possible sounds of these times of day—the awakening of birds, the rising of the sun—but also attempts to depict the moods and emotions attendant on these times of day. Here, almost for the first time, a composer is using the resources of the orchestra to suggest poetic feelings without resorting to words. A century later there would be a name for this: program music. Haydn got there first.

Haydn has been dubbed by some popular historian as "Father of the Symphony." If so, Haydn's paternity is a freak of genetics, so varied were his offspring.

By the time Haydn took up his post at Esterház, a generation of composers before him had clearly established the outlines of a new musical language and, more to the point, the way this language was to follow certain broad structural principles (as outlined in the opening to this chapter). One thing you should always bear in mind, however, when thinking about musical forms in Haydn's time or in any time. No composer worth his salt ever worked with a diagram in front of him prescribing the form his music should take. The principles talked about today as sonata form and the like are, rather, the general tendencies that music followed at the time, and music followed those principles because, to the composer (and to us today) they seemed logical. They supplied a framework within which the language of the time could find expression.

Even so, Haydn made it clear from the start of his career that he was not always prepared to accept these principles if he happened to have a better idea in mind. Did the sonata-form principle state that a new theme should emphasize the change to a second key? Haydn devised any number of movements wherein the same theme does double service in both the first and second key areas. In such instances (the first movement of his very last symphony, No. 104, or the first movement of a particularly attractive earlier symphony, No. 88, are two of many examples), Haydn seems to be using the sonata form as a demonstration of conciseness, of a kind of musical obsessiveness with a single idea and its many permutations, rather than the customary study in contrasts.

Other symphonies, other departures. In place of the usual brilliant opening movement, Haydn began with long, slow movements of a more serious, even somber, mien. The slow first movement of No. 22 has its solemnity enhanced by having the customary oboes in the orchestra replaced by the deeper-voiced English horns; this symphony, for that very reason, has been given the nickname *The Philosopher*. Symphony No. 49, subtitled *The Passion*, also begins with a tragic, slow movement.

In other symphonies Haydn sets out to test the virtuosity of the Esterházy orchestra, creating symphonic movements that almost merge into concertos. Symphony No. 13, for example, has a long and flowing cello solo in its second movement, and No. 31, known as the *Horn Signal*, uses a quartet of French horns that come in as a unit and scatter the brilliant sounds of hunting horns over the symphonic landscape. In the finale of No. 60, Haydn plays one of his famous jokes: the violins are made to retune midway in the movement, and the ensuing racket makes for a moment of unsettling ruckus.

The constant experimentation in this music supplies some of its interest, but the music itself is more interesting yet. Haydn drew much of his melodic inspiration from his Croatian background: not only dance rhythms but also a favorite device of his, setting a tune in the upper part of the orchestra against a held note, or "drone" in the bass, a symphonic imitation of country bagpipes. The finale of Haydn's very last symphony, No. 104, makes extensive use of this device. His melodic style differs from the almost-vocal poigancy of the music of Mozart (whom Haydn revered above all men), but by the end of his symphonic career his music had gained a profundity of utterance second to no composer of the time.

As his mastery deepened, Haydn's music took on a fierce dramatic power. The late symphonies, composed for the London impresario Salomon after Haydn had retired from the Esterházy post, teem with raw orchestral power: sudden fortissimo outbursts, strong accents on unexpected beats, strange and misty harmonic progressions. In his early years in Vienna, the young Beethoven sought out Haydn; the influence of master upon pupil—the line of succession, if you will—is unmistakable.

SELECTED RECORDINGS

Symphonies Nos. 1–104
–Antal Dorati and the Philharmonia Hungarica (complete on forty-six disks) (London/Decca)

Symphonies Nos. 6, 7, and 8 (*Morning, Noon,* and *Evening*)
–Karl Ristenpart and the Saar Chamber Orchestra (Nonesuch)

Symphonies Nos. 12, 26, and 83
–Leslie Jones and the London Little Orchestra (Nonesuch/Pye)

Symphonies Nos. 44 and 49
–Daniel Barenboim and the English Chamber Orchestra (Angel/Deutsche Grammophon)

Symphonies Nos. 82–87 (the "Paris" symphonies)
–Leonard Bernstein and the New York Philharmonic (three disks) (Columbia)

Symphonies Nos. 94 and 96
–Neville Marriner and the Academy of St. Martin-in-the-Fields (Philips)

Symphonies Nos. 99 and 100
–Eugen Jochum and the London Philharmonic Orchestra (Deutsche Grammophon)

Symphonies Nos. 103 and 104
–Eugen Jochum and the London Philharmonic Orchestra (Deutsche Grammophon)

Trumpet Concerto in E flat
–Gerard Schwartz and the YMHA Chamber Symphony of New York (Delos)

Aside from the first entry, the above is a generous but arbitrary sampling. Certainly a complete set of Haydn's 104 symphonies would be a privilege to own, with pleasure and information on every side. Certainly Antal Dorati's performances, using newly edited scores that correct many errors that former generations of conductors had perpetuated, are livelier and more respectful than most of the recorded work by this unevenly talented conductor. Just as certainly, however, a set of forty-six disks represents the cost of several gallons of motor fuel.

Among the chosen single records of Haydn symphonies (two or three to a record), several styles of performance are exemplified in this list. The performances by the late Karl Ristenpart (who, in a brief recording career, even with his not–quite–first-rate orchestra from Saarbrücken, set high standards for elegant chamber-orchestra performances of early music), Leslie Jones, Daniel Barenboim, and Neville Marriner use orchestras about the size (twenty to thirty players) that Haydn himself had to work with at the Esterházy palace. These performances, too, revert to Haydn's own use of the harpsichord as a support for the small orchestral sounds. Although Leonard Bernstein had few successes with pre-1850 music, he did have a fine insight into Haydn's dramatic orchestral writing. (Curiously, Bernstein's recorded Mozart performances were uniformly poor.) And the venerable Eugen Jochum, even with a full-sized orchestra, performs Haydn with a dramatic clarity and nobility of musical line that outweigh his basically old-fashioned approach.

The symphonies themselves represent a wide stylistic variety in Haydn's remarkably inventive style. First comes that early trilogy, with its use of the orchestra as a pictorial force that seems strangely prophetic of music to come. Symphony No. 26 (given the title *Lamentation* by a publisher) is a stark, dramatic piece seemingly akin to the Sturm und Drang poetry of contemporary writers; the companion No. 83 bears the subtitle *The Hen*, because of a sort of "clucking" figuration that forms the contrasting theme in the first movement. Both Nos. 44 (*Funeral*) and 49 (*Passion*) are works of great emotional range. Note especially the long slow movement that begins No. 49 and also, in the third movement, the unusually high notes for the horns, which are passages of extreme difficulty.

The six symphonies written for Paris in 1788, shortly before Haydn's retirement from Esterház, are wonderfully fanciful works. Symphony No. 82, called *The Bear*, has one of Haydn's amusing "drone" effects in its last movement, probably a depiction of a rustic hand-organ of the sort used in trained-bear acts. Symphony No. 86 is a noble work, deeply expressive. Notice particularly its slow movement (in the unusual key of B major—five sharps) with its haunting, elegiac mood.

The twelve symphonies (Nos. 93–104) written for the London concerts of Johann Peter Salomon were the first Haydn scores to be published throughout Europe, and they remain the most popular of his works. In them, Haydn continued to introduce novel effects. Symphony No. 94 is the well-known *Surprise* symphony, so-called for the sudden loud note in the slow movement that Haydn assumed "would make the ladies scream." Symphony No. 99 has another particularly moving slow movement, while No. 100 has no slow movement at all. This is the much-loved *Military* symphony, so-called because the expected slow movement has been replaced by an easy going military march that is suddenly and explosively peppered with such marching-band paraphernalia as bass drum, cymbals, and triangle. Symphony No. 103 is called the *Drumroll*, for reasons apparent in the very first measure. The slow movement is an especially fine set of variations on a theme of great simplicity and seriousness. And the last of the London symphonies is actually known as the *London*, probably because its finale includes an English folktune (introduced over a drone)—Haydn's farewell to his British patron.

The lively and inventive trumpet concerto also dates from the London years; it is the most mature, and successful example of Haydn's relatively meager output in concerto form.

Wolfgang Amadeus Mozart

b Salzburg, Austria, January 27, 1756; *d* Vienna, December 5, 1791. Principal output includes: nearly fifty symphonies (exact number unclear because of possibly spurious works published under Mozart's name); twenty-seven piano concertos; six violin concertos; other concerted works for flute, oboe, clarinet, bassoon, and horn; and a considerable amount of "social" music (serenades, divertimentos) for various instrumental combinations. Also: operas; sacred choral music; chamber music; sonatas for piano and for violin with piano; and songs.

The phenomenon of the child prodigy occurs frequently in music: the child (or adolescent dressed as a child by ambitious parents and/or promoter) who has learned to imitate the mechanical performance abilities of his elders at an exploitably early age. The history of musical prodigies adds up to a mixed account: on the one hand, a pathway strewn with worshipful admirers, sometimes indeed exalted to a state of religious frenzy; on the other, a blighted later existence as the consequence of a warped childhood. Some ex-prodigies, such as the violinists Yehudi Menuhin and Ruggiero Ricci and the conductor Lorin Maazel, have survived into mature musical success, but they are the exceptions, the product of someone older having taken exceptionally good care of a budding talent.

Nobody knows exactly how the 6-year-old Wolfgang Mozart played, his stubby fingers clutching a violin as his older sister Nannerl accompanied at the keyboard, but his father Leopold trundled him across the map of Europe to exhibit his precocity before nobles and crowned heads. We do know that one consequence of this grotesque childhood was a later life somewhat marred by persistent childishness. In the depths of later financial despair, Mozart was incapable of harvesting a sou for the next day's food. But there is evidence at hand that the cherub who ravished the hearts of Europe with his boyish prodigiousness possessed, even in those earliest years, a creative mind that was beyond anyone's power to exploit—anyone, that is, but Mozart himself. There are symphonies by the 9-year-old Mozart, piano pieces from even earlier, and a Kyrie Eleison for chorus and orchestra from his tenth year that are not merely proficient imitations of the music of the time. Each one moved the art of musical expression, however haltingly, to some level that nobody had reached before.

By the time he was 20, Mozart had created a repertoire larger than many have composed in a full lifetime. His orchestral output by 1776 included thirty symphonies, five violin concertos, and countless more or less lightweight pieces—serenades and divertimentos, works usually written on order for one or another nobleman and meant to be played during dinners or social gatherings. That, plus an equally prodigious assortment of music in other forms, served to attract some attention to the adult Mozart as a composer successfully emerged from prodigy status.

Listening to some of these youthful works—the ravishing G-major Violin Concerto, for example, or Symphony No. 20, or the spacious, oratorical Serenade No. 4 (can so eloquent a work really have been conceived as background music?)—can be a powerful experience. You hear quite clearly the formal divisions of the classic musical structure (see page 21) and at the same time you sense the unmistakable presence of a free-spirited creative force whose music flows through those divisions and comes at you as a wordless rhapsody of great emotional power.

The prime influence on Mozart's musical style, from his earliest days, was opera, the way music and words interact to create a kind of drama more powerful than either of its components. Mozart heard Italian opera in his native Salzburg and on his childhood travels. At the age of 14 he wrote letters from Bologna and Mantua in which it is clear that opera had become his most passionate musical obsession. Later, he was to write four masterpieces—*Marriage of Figaro*, *Don Giovanni*, *Così fan tutte*, and *The Magic Flute*—which have never been excelled for the way the power of words and the power of music overcome limitations of time, the confines of a stage, and the inadequacies of individual singers and for the way they reach their audiences with the immediacy of a heartbeat.

But Mozart had that operatic gift even in his instrumental music, and that is what most sets him apart

33

from the other composers of his time. In the first work of his artistic maturity, the Sinfonia Concertante for solo violin and viola with orchestra, you sense at every moment that the two soloists are engaged in ardent conversation between themselves and with the orchestra. The melodies seem to be made out of questions followed by answers.

That work dates from 1779, and it marks a landmark both in Mozart's music and in his life. A few months later he settled in Vienna, where he spent his last years struggling to establish himself as an independent composer, aided by a few close friends but ignored by the majority of the Viennese public. Great as the last symphonies composed in Vienna are, Mozart's orchestral masterpieces from that last decade are the piano concertos that he created, most of them for himself as soloist at concerts paid for out of his own pocket or by as many tickets as he could sell.

In these concertos, especially Nos. 17–25, Mozart brings about a synthesis between the style of orchestral composition and his own obsession with immediate personal expression. The piano in each of these works is like a cast of operatic characters: heroic, brave, and now and then ill-tempered in the fast movements, pleading and seductive in the slow movements. The soloist engages in constant conversation with the orchestra and this, too, undergoes many changes of character. In the D-minor Concerto (No. 20), the orchestra is stormy and rash; in the C-major (No. 21), the constant punctuation of trumpets and timpani gives the music a brave, military quality at first, while in the slow movement the hushed tones of muted strings are totally overpowered by the quasi-vocal melody (much of it a simple, unharmonized, one-finger tune) from the piano. These concertos are extraordinary works; there is nothing else in music quite like them. They are also monstrously difficult to perform, because their virtuosic demands (which are formidable enough) must always be subservient to the "humanness" in the soloist's music.

The final three symphonies, composed during one six-week period in 1788, are an extraordinary summation of classic orchestral writing, and of the emotional breadth that Mozart (and, at the end of his life, Haydn) could draw from within the outlines of classic musical structure. Each of the works is from its own world. The E flat (No. 39) is exceptionally profligate; the work seems to be built out of an endless outpouring of melody, a new one beginning almost before the last has caught its breath. That, and the almost human use of solo wind instruments within the orchestra, give this symphony a warmth that seems to look ahead to the Romantic era. Symphony No. 40 in G minor is stark, spare, classic in the way its passion seems chiseled into stone. Symphony No. 41 in C major, the so-called *Jupiter*, lives up to its nickname in music of broad, almost martial expanse, relieved only in the slow movement by what seems to be an unspoken human tragedy of unbearable poignancy. The finale is a tour de force; here is Mozart, at the culmination of a musical era that had begun with a rejection of the contrapuntal complexity of Bach and the Baroque, paying unwitting homage to the giants of the past in a vast contrapuntal tying-together of five separate themes.

Of those melodies, the one most clearly heard has also appeared as the principal theme in the slow movement of Mozart's very first symphony, twenty-three years earlier.

SELECTED RECORDINGS

Piano Concertos No. 9 in E flat (K. 271) **and No. 21 in C** (K 467)
   –Murray Perahia, soloist and conductor, with the English Chamber Orchestra (Columbia)
Piano Concertos No. 20 in D minor (K. 466) **and No. 23 in A** (K. 488)
   –Stephen Bishop-Kovacevitch, soloist, with Colin Davis and the London Symphony Orchestra (Philips)
Piano Concerto No. 24 in C minor (K. 491)
   –Edwin Fischer, soloist and conductor, with the Danish Chamber Orchestra (also includes Mozart's Symphony No. 35 in D, conducted by Fischer) (Turnabout)
Violin Concertos No. 3 in G (K. 216) **and No. 5 in A** (K. 219)
   –Sophie Mutter, soloist, with Herbert von Karajan and the Berlin Philharmonic Orchestra (Deutsche Grammophon)

Sinfonia Concertante in E flat, for violin, viola, and orchestra (K. 364)

–Isaac Stern and Pinchas Zuckerman, soloists, with Daniel Barenboim and the English Chamber Orchestra (also includes a Sinfonia Concertante by Carl Stamitz) (Columbia)

–Isaac Stern and William Primrose, soloists, with Pablo Casals and the Perpignan Festival Orchestra (Columbia)

Serenade No. 4 in D (K. 203)

–Karl Ristenpart and the Saar Chamber Orchestra (Nonesuch)

Symphonies No. 18 in F (K. 130) **and No. 20 in D** (K. 133)

–Neville Marriner and the Academy of St. Martin-in-the-Fields (Philips)

Symphonies No. 38 in D (K. 504) **and No. 41 in C** (K. 551)

–Colin Davis and the BBC Symphony Orchestra (Philips)

Symphonies No. 39 in E flat (K. 543) **and No. 40 in G minor** (K. 550)

–Colin Davis and the BBC Symphony Orchestra (Philips)

Symphonies No. 40 in G minor (K. 550) **and No. 41 in C** (K. 551)

–Sir Thomas Beecham and the London Philharmonic Orchestra (Vox-Turnabout)

What is that "K" in all the titles? Ludwig von Koechel (1800–77) was an Austrian botanist and Mozart enthusiast who devoted years to cataloguing every work Mozart wrote in chronological order, a job of enormous difficulty since few of the works were published during the composer's lifetime. Koechel's catalogue runs from Nos. 1 to 626; thus, a "K" number indicates where that work stands in Koechel's listing.

How can one ever arrange a "selective" list of Mozart's music, whose every note tells us something different and important? Let the above, then, stand merely as a stepping-off point. A true understanding of this music, furthermore, will come only after you have digested at least one of the operas, and let that be the Marriage of Figaro (in the performance under Colin Davis's direction.)

Even in the amazing works of the very young Mozart, we can hear him working with his instruments as if they were singers in the best and purest sense. This is evident in the wonderful early symphonies—in No. 20 most of all, whose slow movement seems like one long arch of song—and in the splendid range of drama, from boisterous comedy to poignant lyricism, in the set of violin concertos that date from Mozart's late adolescence. Even in the long Serenade (K. 203), the kind of piece all composers had to write on commission for one or another noble festivity, the range of emotion is remarkable; even at his most "disposable," Mozart couldn't evade greatness.

Just to take these early works, and follow an imaginary line from there to the astounding symphonies of the late years—No. 38 (the so-called *Prague*) with its intensely serious slow movement, the marvelous use of clarinets as quasi-human participants in No. 39, the distillation of pure tragedy in No. 40, and the range of majesty in the well-nicknamed *Jupiter*—is to witness the most extraordinary unfolding of artistic mastery in the entire realm of music. The conductor who would realize the nature of this music must value that mastery as a living quality, not as something out of the museum. The performances listed here come close.

Murray Perahia is one of the best young Mozartian pianists, and his added talent in being able to conduct his own performances preserves the dramatic give-and-take that is crucial in this music. Yet Davis and the American-born Bishop-Kovacevitch also work together as one. The Danish recording by Edwin Fischer dates back to the mid-1940s, but this venerable pianist was one of the first in this century to rescue Mozart's music from the tendency of Victorian musicians to romanticize and misrepresent all music of the 18th century. (Sir Thomas Beecham also did yeoman work in this regard, which is why his old but noble recording of two of the symphonies is also included here.)

The key to the astounding Sinfonia Concertante of 1779 is the somber, prophetic slow movement; it must be played neither daintily (as by some violinists in quest of "authenticity") nor romantically. Stern has captured the essence in his two recordings; the old one, with William Primrose conducted by Casals in 1951, is a treasure worth ransacking secondhand shops to find. On the newer Stern recording, however, is a work by Carl Stamitz, one of Mozart's forbears, which will suggest how tall Mozart's music stood above the craft of his thousands of contemporaries.

SUPPLEMENTARY COMPOSERS

Johann Christian Bach (1735–1782)
Sinfonias No. 3 and No. 5; Sinfonia Concertante
  –Leslie Jones and the Little Orchestra (Nonesuch)
Harpsichord Concerto in A major
  –George Malcolm, soloist, with Neville Marriner and the Academy of St. Martin-in-the-Fields (London)

Carl Philipp Emanuel Bach (1714–1788)
Flute Concerto; Cello Concerto
  –Various soloists with Pierre Boulez and the Paris Chamber Orchestra (Oryx)
Orchestral Symphonies in D major, E - flat major, F major, and G major
  –Leslie Jones and the Little Orchestra (Nonesuch)

Giovanni Battista Sammartini (1701–1775)
Six Symphonies for Orchestra
  –Newell Jenkins and the Angelicum Orchestra of Milan (Nonesuch)

Luigi Boccherini (1743–1805)
Cello Concerto in D major; Concerto for Cello and Two Horns in C major
  –Amsterdam Chamber Orchestra (Telefunken)
Six Symphonies
  –Raymond Leppard and the New Philharmonia Orchestra (Philips)

Leopold Mozart (1719–1787)
Musical Sleighride; Peasant Wedding
  –Eduard Melkus and a chamber ensemble (with toy instruments) (Deutsche Grammophon)

Until the great rediscovery of the music of Johann Sebastian Bach in the 19th century, the name Bach was
more likely to mean the youngest of Sebastian's sons,
Johann Christian, who settled in London and founded
one of that city's first public concert halls. He composed copiously in a style that marked the high-water
line of the graceful, elegant Rococo, a reaction against
the complexities in his father's music. The child Mozart came to London during J. C. Bach's time, and the
legend of the elder composer greatly encouraging the
toddling genius is well founded.

Carl Philipp Emanuel, twenty-one years senior to
Johann Christian, settled in Berlin, where he lived in
the currents of the growing German literary expression, particularly the passionate Sturm und Drang
movement of the younger writers. Some of this passion for passion got into his music (as it did, indeed,
into some of Haydn's early symphonies and even the
works, such as the first Piano Sonata, of the young
Beethoven).

In Italy, the generations after the Baroque string
composers also produced many talented composers
whose music mirrored the trend toward elegance, simplicity, and lively tunefulness. Sammartini's orchestral
works were enormously popular throughout Europe; it
is likely that the young Mozart was somewhat
touched by the clarity and grace of this writing. The
prolific Boccherini, an adept string player himself,
composed in virtually every known form. His style
has a soft, feminine sweetness; the familiar "Minuet,"
from one of his string quintets, contains the "essential" Boccherini. One critic has referred to him (or, at
least, his musical self) as "Haydn's wife." If you set
aside the amatory implications, the term is accurate.

The elder Mozart, mentioned here, was a violinist,
author of several important musical treatises still being
studied, and a reasonably proficient composer in and
around Salzburg. His most famous piece, the *Musical
Sleighride*, is of a genre much liked at the time: orchestral music that includes toy or mechanical instruments. But when the charm of Leopold's music has
been assimilated, it still remains clear that his greatest
creation was his son.

The Time of Transition

The time, for the sake of argument, was 1810. Joseph Haydn had died in Vienna the year before, honored and mourned throughout the musical world. Mozart, twenty-four years Haydn's junior, and dubbed by Haydn as "the greatest composer known to me," had been dead for nearly two decades, his passing little noted and even his burial place unmarked. Yet Mozart's music was still performed, more frequently and to greater acclaim than in his lifetime. Walking home from hearing Mozart's C-minor Piano Concerto at a concert, Ludwig van Beethoven said to a friend, "Alas, we will never do as well."

Music had become firmly entrenched in middle-class society, which had invaded the precincts of the nobility many decades before in the first public concert halls. London boasted several symphony orchestras, which kept alive the memory of Haydn's visits to that capital and also played the new works from the Continent, including all the latest Beethoven. Paris, Munich, Leipzig, Dresden, Warsaw, and St. Petersburg—all maintained their opera and their symphony, nourished constantly by major scores, played while the ink was barely dry. The musical taste of the time was for the latest novelty, and the public hunger sometimes outran the traditional dour conservatism of the critics, one of whom found in the Second Symphony of Beethoven "subversive" elements against which young people should be warned.

By 1810 nearly every bourgeois household boasted a pianoforte, in the place of honor that would be occupied by today's television set. After dinner the guests would repair to the music room; out of every social gathering there were bound to be enough musicians for an impromptu session of chamber music or songs at the piano. One learned the symphonic masterpieces of the day by performing them in abridged arrangements (usually made by the composer himself) for home chamber music groups.

Beethoven was 40 in 1810, and had composed his first six symphonies and all of his concertos. He had come to Vienna when he was 21, because it was, above all cities, the music capital. The aging Haydn had taken him on for a few lessons. Mozart, practically on his deathbed, had predicted that the newcomer "would make a noise in the world." Even· so, the noise was not always heard, even in Vienna. Until his final years of adulation, Beethoven had to compete for favor with the popular passion for Italian opera, most of all Italian comic opera—the work of lesser composers like Domenico Cimarosa and Giovanni Paisiello and later of the genius in the genre, Gioacchino Rossini. The Viennese public hungered after music, which it seemed to lap up at times with the same avidity as it showed for the sour new wine of the local vineyards. In both cases, however, the quality of Viennese taste did not match the expanse of Viennese appetite. Mozart had also found this out when he was obliged to add slapstick elements to his powerful and serious *Don Giovanni* before it could earn favor in Vienna.

In 1810, too, another musician was growing up in Vienna, this one native-born. Franz Peter Schubert was 13, and had already written some startling, dramatic songs and a few charming, if aimless, pieces of chamber music. He, too, soon discovered that the public taste for happy, uncomplicated Italian melody tended to make the going hard for composers with serious intent.

For all its overall conservatism, however, Vienna still maintained the climate in which musical greatness could flourish. There was something in the grand old city—perhaps nothing more than the quality of its food and drink, plus the foulness of its climate, which suggested the great indoors as the normal scene of activity—that stimulated creativity. From the turn of the 18th century almost until the outbreak of the First World War, the sovereign portion of the world's best music was created within earshot of St. Stephen's mighty cathedral.

The composers who worked in Vienna in the first decades of the new century—Beethoven and Schubert, most of all—had ready access to the glories of recent tradition. Mozart and Haydn were living memories, as were the hundreds of lesser figures who also scribbled out symphonies and concertos. It was easy for a genius with a mind of sublime restlessness to sense that in the final works of the two classic masters an outlook on artistic creation had more or less reached its zenith. The feeling was all around that new artistic beginnings were needed—not only because of the start of a new century but also because of more immediate matters like the onrush of the Napoleonic juggernaut.

Both Beethoven and Schubert spent their early years steeped in the traditions of Vienna's recent past. Both began their symphonic work somewhat under the shadow of the classic symphonic style, although the first symphonies of both composers are stamped distinctively with the fingerprints of their creators. Sooner or later, each composer came, in his symphonic style, to a time of personal explosion: Beethoven, in 1805, in the *Eroica*, possibly the most daring single forward step in the history of Western culture, and Schubert, in 1822, in the B-minor Symphony, which reached toward such far expressive horizons that the composer himself feared for his power to cope with it and laid it aside unfinished.

Music historians long ago conveniently evolved the term "Romantic" to describe the musical style of the 19th century. The epithet makes sense, in terms of a growing entente between music and poetry, and of the tendency in music to forswear the sublime balance of classic structure in favor of the overt depiction of personal emotion. And finally, in terms of two contradictory tendencies: of music becoming grander in scope and in variety of sound, and also becoming small and expressive of great intimacy.

Scarcely a year separates Schubert's *Unfinished* symphony and Beethoven's Ninth—opposite ends of the rainbow—both written in Vienna.

Much of what came to be regarded as Romantic

traits in music took shape in the works of Beethoven and Schubert. Yet, what can be said of such music as the slow movement of Mozart's C-major Piano Concerto (K. 467)—the movement given undeserved notoriety by its use in a movie called *Elvira Madigan*? Does any music go farther toward sheer, unbridled expressiveness than this haunting eight minutes of the most intimate communication? Is this where Romanticism actually began? Then what about the slow movement of Bach's first "Brandenburg" Concerto or the "Crucifixus" from his B-minor Mass?

This is all to point up the danger of convenient journalistic labels. By whatever name, however, the world's music evolved during the years of Beethoven and of his near-contemporary Schubert to become far different in sound and intent from the way it had been before.

Ludwig van Beethoven

b Bonn, December 16, 1770; *d* Vienna, March 27, 1827. Principal output includes: nine symphonies; five piano concertos, a violin concerto, and one for violin, cello, piano, and orchestra; concert overtures and incidental music to plays; the opera *Fidelio*; two masses and several other choral works; thirty-two piano sonatas, ten sonatas for violin and piano, five for cello and piano; seventeen string quartets and numerous other chamber works; songs; and early orchestral, choral, and chamber works of little besides historical importance.

The beginnings were modest at best: an acceptably talented adolescent in a provincial and conservative metropolis, his father a minor court musician (who drank to compensate for his artistic insignificance), his mother a good-hearted, uneducated peasant. Teachers in Bonn found the young Beethoven worth the trouble to instruct in musical rudiments, and he repaid their efforts with a few proficient pieces, including a piano concerto, that reflected careful observation of the style of the time. His more impressive skill, that of a master improviser at the piano, earned him somewhat more attention, and, in 1787, the young man was sent to make a name for himself in the only place where a musical name meant anything: Vienna. (The trip was financed by a certain Bonn nobleman, Count Ferdinand Waldstein, whose name lives on as the dedicatee of Beethoven's C-major Piano Sonata, Opus 53.)

In Vienna, Beethoven was heard with admiration by Mozart, but circumstances forced his return to Bonn. There, in 1793, five years later, he was heard by the great Joseph Haydn, who passed through the city on his way home from his triumphant engagement in London, and it was Haydn who urged the 22-year-old musician to return to Vienna, this time for good. Once in Vienna, Beethoven found friendship, patronage, and tutelage at Haydn's side, and at that moment he publicly disowned whatever music he had composed up to that time. (Not quite, actually: a long aria from a cantata on the death of Joseph II, written at Bonn in 1790, found its way, virtually unaltered, into the score of the later opera *Fidelio*, where it sublimely underscores the most moving moment in the entire opera, as the heroine Leonora unlocks the chains that bind her husband who she has heroically rescued.)

Haydn's influence was crucial to Beethoven's own developing outlook. There was throughout Haydn's career a continual implied challenge to the overtly rigid structural aesthetic of late classicism: a constant struggle, sometimes whimsical and just as often dramatic, to see how far the letter of the rules could be stretched without doing violence to their spirit. We cannot know exactly what kind of lessons Haydn gave his protégé, but it's easy to suspect that they included the mandate "dare." And so, in the first measure of his first symphony, written in 1799, Beethoven's daring takes him at least one step beyond Haydn's own boundaries of adventure: rather than clearly stating his chosen key of C major, Beethoven starts off with a wriggly passage of purposely blurred harmony that makes it anyone's guess what key he's in. (A quarter-century later, Beethoven would begin his Ninth Symphony in even more baffling harmonic ambiguity, a cloudy passage so opposed to classic harmonic practice that its exact meaning is still argued today.)

It is a truism in the arts that the innovators are rarely the geniuses—that the artist who takes the great forward leap must then defer to the others who will explore the consequences of that leap. That can be proven here and there in music; the first operas composed after the form was invented (around 1600) were pretty pokey stuff, and so were the first symphonies in the new classic style in the 18th century. Yet, it can be disproven with equal vigor—by such works as Richard Wagner's mature musical dramas, by Igor Stravinsky's *Rite of Spring*, and, with greater triumph yet, by almost every one of the nine symphonies of Beethoven.

The first two (1799 and 1802) were, to be sure, broadly couched in careful observation of what had worked for Haydn and Mozart—a nice balancing of unity and contrast within movements and from one to the next, with the finale tending toward an undemanding brilliance to reward the crowd for its twenty-four minutes or so of attention. Yet, even here, the innovator, the unruly revolutionary, is struggling to break through; listen to the jarring contrasts, the rude orchestral outbursts, in the finale of the Second Symphony for a pretty good foretaste of what was to come.

What came was, in 1805, the Third Symphony, the *Sinfonia Eroica*, whose first purpose had been to honor the heroism of the once-idolized Napoleon Bonaparte. Two hammerblows on E-flat chords establish the tonality of the opening, in true classic style, and so do the first few notes of the first theme itself, the mere outline of the basic E-flat harmony (a melodic shape, in fact, which the child Mozart had used to begin his very first opera). But that melody takes a cataclysmic turn, nine notes in, to a note totally unrelated to its context, and it will take a phenomenal outpouring of energy to right this wrong. And so Beethoven draws us into a struggle of gigantic proportion to redress his own transgression, an interlocking of musical design and emotional emanation that sweeps past all "normal" outlines that music had easily observed before this time. Rhythms are violently displaced through huge chains of offbeat accentuations that leave the actual time scale obscured. Melodic material exists first as tiny fragments that seem to grow as we listen. Then midway in the development there is a harmonic pileup of ever more terrifying dissonance, until, at the point where no more seems bearable, an entirely new melody intrudes as yet another surprise. Only after this gigantic movement has run nearly fifteen minutes—twice the length of any previous symphonic movement—does Beethoven reveal the true shape of that diabolically deceptive opening gambit. The whole movement has been a breath-stopping, steady progression toward that one climactic revelation.

And there were three movements yet to come: the second, a "funeral march" that moves in somber tread, blazes into triumph now and then, but subsides finally into a musical language of such palpable, monumental sadness as almost to demand words. An ensuing short scherzo relaxes the demands upon the audience momentarily, but then comes a titanic finale, a vast departure once again from the classic notion of the merely happy simple ending. Here a melody seems to materialize from a vast distance away, treading slowly toward us a quiet step at a time. It finally materializes, then becomes the basis for a wildly contrasting set of variations. There is a fading–off toward the end, a grandiose peroration, and a final exhilarating rush through the orchestra caps this enormous, daring conception. In this single forward leap, Beethoven shatters, then triumphantly rebuilds in the image of his own colossal artistry, the institution of the symphony.

In their implied acceptance or rejection of Beethoven's own mandate—to explode, to rebuild, to take no prior precept as law—every one of the ensuing symphonies is some kind of progression. The Fifth and Seventh are vital explorations in obsession, in the way the tiniest musical nugget (a melodic shape, a rhythmic figure) can generate vast symphonic structures. The Sixth, the *Pastoral*, postulates a whole new way that music can serve—not as the exact counterpart, but as a generative force within the hearer's imagination—as the handmaiden of visual stimulus; the calculated monotony of the first two movements and finale, for example, tell us as much about the spirituality of rural life as the more literal dance and thunderstorm

46

episodes in the middle. The Fourth and Eighth symphonies seem slighter at first observation, but they are still extraordinarily daring, in their way of adapting Beethoven's own iconoclasm to a kind of revisited classic form.

What is the most remarkable, as we try as best we can to trace the vast and continued outburst of Beethoven's own growth, is not merely the stature of the music, but of the deepening sense of involvement of Beethoven himself in his music. He was, after all, the first composer to spend the major part of his life as a free artist, free, that is, in the sense that no single patron kept him on salary with the job of turning out works continually. Mozart, late in life, had walked away from patronage to try life as a public artist, and he didn't get very far. Beethoven, however, did just that for all his mature life. He lived as every composer since his time has lived, locked in the demeaning process of courting the public, courting impresarios and publishers, building a public image simply in order to eat. This changed lifestyle served to force any composer to live in far closer relationship to his own work than ever before, to come to grips with such Romantic concepts as "message" and "posterity."

Any mature work of Beethoven, therefore, reveals a great deal more of the man himself than we might meet in even the most profound work by Mozart (who could, after all, create the joyous *Magic Flute* during his final weeks of sickness and poverty). And, in a sense, the drama that underscores his climactic symphonic work, the Ninth Symphony, has to be taken as both a personal and an artistic struggle. A gigantic struggle that seems at first to coalesce at a vast remove from a void in which harmony and melody have no form and rhythm scarcely exists, that moves from there through the ebb and flow of a floodtide of sometimes grotesque forms, some murky and others radiant, to the point, finally, where the struggle simply demands a new dimension. And so, as the last movement begins, the separate instruments of the orchestra take on the role of discussants, some pleading for something new and some impatiently rejecting all pleas. All that can be left is to set words to the struggle, and so Beethoven's four vocal soloists and huge chorus join and prolong the battle—the music's battle, the composer's own battle—in the only way remaining, with a vast vocal panorama, using Friedrich Schiller's "Ode to Joy."

The Ninth cast its shadow over music for decades, arguably even to the present time. Its implied drama, the sense it carries of a horizon pleading to be revealed, strongly influenced the Romantic definition of music that took shape throughout the 19th century. Its opening, an idea gradually taking its form from out of the clouds and seeming to come at the listener from vast distances, became virtually the stock cliché of the Romantics, painters no less than composers. The list of later works that began that way is as long as patience allows: Wagner's *Ring*, all nine of Anton Bruckner's symphonies and several of Mahler's, Richard Strauss's *Thus Spake Zarathustra*, Stravinsky's *Firebird*, and on and on. No later composer, however, ever dared to try to emulate the drama that Beethoven achieved in his finale.

The symphonies span Beethoven's career, but even so, their range of innovation is only part of the furious outbreak of the man's artistry. The string quartets cover an equal time span, and the intimacy of their musical language allowed Beethoven to voice his personal dramatic visions in softer, subtler tones. So did the marvelous series of piano sonatas, thirty-two in all, with the last one dying off into silence with questions left unanswered that no genius since has answered. Among the other orchestral works there are the five grand piano concertos, the first two predating the First Symphony and the last two coming from Beethoven's ripest middle years. In the finest of these, the Fourth, the entire slow movement seems to hover on the brink of words, a kind of argument between soloist and orchestra in which the soft but soaring voice of the piano wins an impressive victory. Yet, this music, again like nothing that anyone had written before, predated the Ninth Symphony by two full decades.

SELECTED RECORDINGS

Symphonies Nos. 1–9
  –Bernard Haitink and the London Philharmonic Orchestra (Philips)
  –Bruno Walter and the Columbia Symphony Orchestra (Columbia-Odyssey)

Symphonies No. 1 in C major and No. 2 in D major
  –Hans Schmidt-Isserstedt and the Vienna
Philharmonic Orchestra (London/Decca)
Symphony No. 3 in E-flat major
  –Carlo Maria Giulini and the Los Angeles
Philharmonic Orchestra (Deutsche Grammophon)
  –Herbert von Karajan and the Berlin Philharmonic

Orchestra (Deutsche Grammophon)
Symphony No. 4 in B flat
  –Wilhelm Furtwängler and the Vienna
Philharmonic Orchestra (EMI)
Symphony No. 5 in C minor
  –Carlos Kleiber and the Vienna Philharmonic
Orchestra (Deutsche Grammophon)
Wilhelm Furtwängler and the Vienna Philharmonic
Orchestra (EMI)
Symphony No. 6 in F major
  –Hans Schmidt-Isserstedt and the Vienna
Philharmonic Orchestra (London/Decca)
  –Bruno Walter and the Vienna Philharmonic
Orchestra (Turnabout or EMI)
Symphony No. 7 in A major
  –Arturo Toscanini and the New York
Philharmonic-Symphony Orchestra (RCA)
Symphonies No. 8 in F major and No. 9 in D minor
  –Carlo Maria Giulini and the London Symphony
Orchestra (with soloists and chorus in the Ninth)
(Angel)
Piano Concertos Nos. 1–5
  –Vladimir Ashkenazy, pianist, with Georg Solti
and the Chicago Symphony Orchestra
(London/Decca)
  –Artur Schnabel, pianist, with Malcolm Sargent
and the London Philharmonic Orchestra (EMI)
  –Stephen Bishop-Kovacevitch, pianist, with Colin
Davis and the BBC Symphony Orchestra (Philips)
Piano Concerto No. 3 in C minor
  –Solomon, pianist, with Herbert Menges and the
Philharmonia Orchestra (Angel-Seraphim)
Violin Concerto in D major
  –Henryk Szeryng, violinist, with Bernard Haitink
and the Concertgebouw Orchestra (Philips)
Overtures (*Leonora* Nos. 1, 2, 3; *Fidelio*)
  –Otto Klemperer and the Philharmonia Orchestra
(Angel-Seraphim)

First, all the symphonies and concertos listed in the complete albums are also available as single records. This is important, because it stands to reason that in a repertoire as varied as the span of the nine Beethoven symphonies, or the five piano concertos, no single performer's outlook is going to satisfy the demands of all the music or of all the listeners. Haitink's performances of the symphonies are spacious and leisurely, finely lyrical but soft of accent where an overt dramatic sense might seem more in order. Thus, the Haitink version of the *Pastoral* (No. 6) is eminently fine, although the two Viennese performances (one recent and one, the Walter, dating back to 1936) have a loving quality that becomes unforgettable. The complete album under Bruno Walter has a great and noble eloquence, although the orchestra (a pickup group of Hollywood studio players) is not as responsive as was the Vienna Philharmonic of old.

The two single recordings of the *Eroica* (No. 3) are about as far apart in spirit as authoritative approaches to any music could be: Giulini's slow but inexorably gripping, and Karajan's fleet and vital. Let the choice between them be your own Rorschach test; a true Beethovenian would own both these performances, plus several more, so elusive is this music.

The mysticism of Furtwängler's Beethoven, the sense of drama somehow transmuted to granite, is something you can practically touch in the recordings of the Fourth and Fifth he made in Vienna. (But do not confuse them with inferior radio-broadcast performances from Berlin now circulating on cheap labels.) Yet, the young Kleiber's Fifth is also almost unbearably dramatic, an unforgettable rendition. The Vienna Philharmonic performance (under the eloquent Schmidt-Isserstedt) of the first two symphonies also has a fine grasp of the young composer's style as it emerged from the shadow of his musical ancestors.

The Toscanini-Beethoven legend dies hard, but the sad fact remains that his best-known recordings, with the NBC Symphony Orchestra under inferior conditions, were also made when the conductor was in his eighties, his conducting almost like a living mask. The closest we can come to Toscanini's real quality is in the few surviving records he made with the only orchestra that was truly "his," the New York Philharmonic. The Beethoven Seventh dates from 1936; the recording is ancient, but the motivating spirit flames like a beacon. With a little imagination, one might extrapolate from this recording what a vintage Toscanini Ninth might have been like. The wise, noble passion of the Giulini performance comes very close.

Arthur Schnabel was a Beethoven scholar—you might almost say a philosopher—whose playing of the music was very much the center of a cult. Yet listening to the visionary performances of the concertos that he recorded twice in his lifetime shows that the cult had validity. There are two sets of Schnabel recordings of the concertos, both reissued at one time or another and both probably not easy to locate. Either one is worth having; the set with Malcolm Sargent, recorded in the early 1930s, is the earlier and better. Passion and great flair illuminate the work of Ashkenazy with Solti and his marvelous orchestra; the Bishop-Kovacevitch performances with Colin Davis are more introspective, but every bit as revealing.

The great British pianist who used the single name Solomon had a small but loyal following until a stroke in the mid-1950s cut short his career; now that his records are again available this following should grow, because Solomon's playing has a strength and a keenness that seem to aim directly at the heart of whatever he plays. Even though his recordings are old and monaural, at least one performance ought to be in every representative collection.

The Violin Concerto has its splendors, although the best performances are usually less concerned with its "Beethoven–ness" than with the geniality, the relaxation (even at the cost of perhaps one repetition too many), and the amusing insignificance of its very small-scale last movement. Szeryng's straightforward manner may lack the panache of eminent virtuosos who have recorded the work in the past (Jascha Heifetz most notably), but it is in lovely tune with the music itself.

For his one opera, *Fidelio*, Beethoven composed four overtures, none of which were played when the opera was presented in its final revision in 1814! One reason is that the overtures themselves are so imposing—especially Nos. 2 and 3, which are almost like nonvocal summaries of the opera—that they almost overshadow the ensuing music. On their own, these are thrilling works, and the massive Klemperer performances, of all his Beethoven recordings, are amazingly intense.

Franz Peter Schubert

b Vienna, January 31, 1797; *d* Vienna, November 19, 1828. **Principal output includes: symphonies, seven completed, two left incomplete, several movements sketched but left incomplete; concert overtures; suites of incidental music; dances; eight operas (plus sketches and incomplete works); six masses and other choral music for church and concert; chamber music, including fifteen string quartets; a copious quantity of piano music and music for piano four-hands, including several sonatas and other large-scale works; works for vocal ensemble with piano; and over 600 songs.**

Schubert and Mozart are interesting subjects for speculation: the two most spontaneous geniuses in music, living in Vienna a few decades apart, both uncannily talented from an early age and both fated to die in poverty at an early age. Even so, the death of Mozart at 36 ended a career that, in its own way, had come full circle, and the music of Mozart's last year—*The Magic Flute* and the Requiem especially—can be viewed as autumnal creations, preternaturally wise for the age of their creator. Schubert's death at 31, on the other hand, took the composer at the moment when he had somehow acquired the answers to artistic questions that had plagued most of his short life.

The predominant question concerned his existence as a composer of large-scale instrumental music, and, by extension, the nature of the artistic horizons that this kind of repertoire faced. During the years of his early adolescence, he employed his ordinary but thorough training in classic musical precepts to jot down some aimless fragments of chamber music and some fully thought-out and original songs. But even then, it is evident that Schubert had found inside himself a seemingly inexhaustible fund of powerful, supple melody and a daring command of harmonic change to give this melody shape and dramatic surprise. By the time he was 20, Schubert's song output numbered over 400, and a handful of them had made their way in the world.

Where the struggle came, however, was in the bending of this melodic fecundity to fit the shapes of classic orchestral works as they were commonly defined in Vienna at the time. As a young man, Schubert created six symphonies (only three of which he was to hear)—lovely works and, in the case of No. 4, works of some passion. They all suffer to some degree, however, from the incompatibility between the soaring, unfettered lyricism of their material and the young composer's assumed need to bend his materials into the dramatic structures that Mozart and Haydn had used so well, and that, even as Schubert wrote, Beethoven so explosively restated. These works are heard today, in the form their beauty demands, but the only acceptable performances embody a total forbearance of the fact that their composer, once he has stated his material, seldom can find much to do with it beyond stating it again. If you think this is, of itself, bad, think again; listen to a considerate performance of the jog-trotting finale to No. 6, for example, and ask yourself if you would willingly spare a single literal repetition.

By 1820, Schubert had come to have a glimmer of how to cope with his own glory. (And it is significant, of course, that from that year on, the output of songs dwindled to a respectable couple–dozen a year, while the instrumental output increased.) There is an unfinished symphony in E major, from 1821, in a British archive, with all four movements fully sketched but not orchestrated. The dramatic impulse in this music (which exists today in completions by others) is a major step forward from the classic orientation of the first six symphonies.

Then, in 1822, came another unfinished work—two movements completed, a third begun—laid aside and not even rediscovered until forty-three years later. That work is now well known, and what we have of it is perfect. It is a work that stands at—no, crosses—the threshold of another musical world, in which harmony extraordinarily used, lyricism that touches the heart, and the orchestra as a source of total, poignant, exultant drama conspire to create a new kind of symphony. Why, then, did Schubert lay the work aside? Simply because, as a desperately poor musician virtually ignored in his native city, he could not afford the time or energy to create music that was ahead of his time. Not once in his pathetically short life did Schubert enjoy the luxury of pure, speculative creation.

Four years later, in 1826, Schubert created his final symphony, not speculatively, but with the probably unrealistic hope of attracting the notice of the august Philharmonic Society. There is no real evidence, however, that anyone of importance ever saw the work during Schubert's lifetime, and this final symphony—No. 9 in the enumeration that includes both unfinished works—was heard first only eleven years after Schubert's death, under the baton of Felix Mendelssohn in Leipzig. (The popular story, by the way, that the Ninth was actually a work of Schubert's final year, 1828, has now been disproven by some scholarly sleuthing.)

There is no work in the repertoire quite like the Ninth. In raising the curtain on a new musical world, it stands as companion and complement to the *Unfinished*, although that can hardly have been Schubert's intent. The outlines are those of classic form, grandly expanded by a cocky self-confidence that allows the simplest material to meander meaningfully through vast and cloudy harmonic spaces. It is a symphony and, at the same time, a drama. Trombones, softly and mysteriously played, punctuate the first movement with questions that nobody in the orchestra can answer; a brave but mournful little march in the slow movement is magically called to order by a solo horn that seems to filter down on a moonbeam track. A motif of nothing more than four repeated notes, first whispered and ultimately roared, tries constantly but in vain to stem the dizzy pace of the finale.

Two major symphonies, then, constitute the total of Schubert's gift to orchestral progress. Yet these two works embody the musical thinking that was already urging the language forward into new realms. Musical Romanticism, after all, lived off the ready rapport be-

tween the musician and the poet, each with his own
view of infinity. The young man who lived among poets, who had already found the music to make 400 and
more of their lyrics live above their own modest
selves, finally in his late years found the way to bring
that poetic sensitivity to music without words. He created, in his last year, three piano sonatas and a string
quintet in which the poetic flame burns dazzlingly.
The mind wonders and the heart breaks to think of
what another year might have brought.

SELECTED RECORDINGS

Symphonies Nos. 1, 2, 3, 4, 5, 6, 8, 9
 –Wolfgang Sawallisch and the Dresden State
 Orchestra (Philips)
**Symphonies No. 5 in B-flat major and No. 6 in
C major**
 –Peter Maag and the Philharmonia Hungarica
 (Turnabout)
**Symphonies No. 4 in C minor and No. 8 in
B minor**
 –Carlo Maria Giulini and the Chicago Symphony
 Orchestra (Deutsche Grammophon)
Symphony No. 7 in E major
 –Franz Litschauer and the Vienna State Opera
 Orchestra (Vanguard)
Symphony No. 9 in C major
 –Carlo Maria Giulini and the Chicago Symphony
 Orchestra (Deutsche Grammophon)
 –Wilhelm Furtwängler and the Berlin Philharmonic
 Orchestra (Deutsche Grammophon)

There is a lovely, easygoingness in both the Sawallisch
and Maag performances, a projection of the feeling
that the music can only make its point at its own
timescale, that makes their performances valuable and
constantly refreshing. Sawallisch's performances are
not available on single records, but the five-record album is in a low-priced series. Litschauer's recording of
the E-major Symphony, in the completion by Felix
Weingartner recorded in 1934, is listed here for the
luckily serendipitous; the record has been out of the
catalogues for years, and there is no other performance
of this fascinating, transitional score.
 Guilini's Schubert recordings are gorgeously played

by the Chicago Symphony, as is Furtwängler's of the Ninth by the Berlin Philharmonic. Both are extremely individualistic approaches, fully aware of the forward-looking quality in this music, both willing to take chances. They are fully successful, but do, admittedly, take some getting used to.

SUPPLEMENTARY COMPOSERS

Juan Christosomo Arriaga (1806–1826)
Symphony in D minor; Overture to Los Esclavos Felices

–Jesús López-Cobos and the English Chamber Orchestra (HNH/Pye)

Luigi Cherubini (1760–1842)
Symphony in D major

–Arturo Toscanini and the NBC Symphony Orchestra (RCA)

Johann Nepomuk Hummel (1778–1837)
Piano Concerto in A minor; Concerto for Violin and Piano

–Various soloists with Martin Galling and the Stuttgart Philharmonic Orchestra (Turnabout)

Trumpet Concerto in E major

–Gerard Schwarz, soloist and conductor, and a chamber orchestra (also includes Haydn's Trumpet Concerto) (Delos)

Ludwig Spohr (1784–1859)
Various works for Violin and Orchestra; Concerto No. 8 and the Grand Potpourri from the opera *Jessonda*

–Susi Lautenbacher, soloist, with a chamber orchestra (Turnabout)

Clarinet Concerto in C minor

–Gervase de Peyer, soloist, with Colin Davis and the London Symphony Orchestra (also includes Weber's Clarinet Concerto in E flat major (Oiseau Lyre)

Carl Maria von Weber (1786–1826)
Clarinet Concerto in E-flat major
  –(see above under Spohr)
**Piano Concertos Nos. 1 and 2; Symphonies Nos. 1
and 2; Overture and March from the incidental
music to Gozzi's Turandot**
  –Malcolm Frager, soloist, with various conductors
  and orchestras (two-record album) (RCA)

The five composers listed here were all active during
the time of Beethoven and Schubert. All, therefore,
coped, consciously or not, with the matter of reconcil-
ing the overtly rigid tenets of classic musical structure,
in which they had all been carefully schooled, with
the free expressiveness of the Romanticism that was in
the air. All failed to some extent; the discrepancy in
their music between the soaring line and the need to
come down to make a proper cadence is something we
hear with amused tolerance today.

But we hear other things, too. In the concertos of
Hummel (a close friend of Beethoven), Spohr, and
most of all, Weber, we hear clearly the beginnings of
something dear to the heart of Romanticism: the passionate melody expressed with transcendent virtuosity
by a "singing" solo instrument (clarinet or violin best
of all). Within not many more years, Frederic Chopin
was to turn this kind of music into the most communi-
cative solo piano style anyone has devised.

Everything in this list, therefore, is music of extraordinary attractiveness, hampered from achieving
greatness only by the fear of its composers—let's not
call it inability—to move onward as decisively as Beethoven and, in his last years, Schubert were able to do.
But there is such individual excellence in this music—
most of all in the music by Weber, although his true
originality came out better in his operas—that all of it
deserves a place in the repertoire. Perhaps the most remarkable is that of the Spaniard Juan Arriaga, who in
his brief lifetime, all of it in Spain except for a few
months' study in Paris, could never have heard a note
by anyone then active in central Europe, certainly not
by Schubert. Yet his one symphony solves problems
in exactly the way the young Schubert was solving
them, and with music of such innate attractiveness
that it deserves to be thought of as "Schubertian."

Romanticism

When Ludwig van Beethoven died in 1827, Frederic Chopin was already creating his first piano works in his native Poland. In 1830, three years after Beethoven's death, Victor Hugo wrote his *Hernani* and Hector Berlioz composed his *Symphonie Fantastique*. The great era of Italian *bel canto* reached its climax with Vincenzo Bellini's *Norma* in 1831. Robert Schumann created his *Symphonic Études* in 1834. A year later Franz Liszt completed the first set of his *Years of Pilgrimage*, and Chopin, now in Paris, published his Opus 25 *Études*.

Just as the early exuberance of the classic style was promulgated while Johann Sebastian Bach was still creating his cantatas in stodgy old Leipzig, the new artistic language of the 19th century took shape while Beethoven, with fierce originality, extracted the last virtues from the musical aesthetic of his immediate forbears, Mozart and Haydn.

The new era called itself Romanticism—as usual, a term from outside the world of music. It had to be considered a Romantic era in every sense. The poets and novelists began it, with their romances of about the romantic, ie, exotic, lands that nobody in Europe had yet seen: Goethe with his *East-West Divan* (whose songs Schubert had set to music); James Fenimore Cooper with his *Leatherstocking Tales* (which Schubert devoured on his deathbed and dreamed of turning into an opera); the mystical poet Jean Paul Richter with his evocation of starry Persian skies; the fake but fragrant Nordic folk poetry of the so-called *Ossian* and the possibly more genuine folk ballads of the *Youth's Magic Horn*. Small wonder, with the artistic world swept with such immensely, immediately appealing writing, that musicians also became obsessed with the idea of infusing meaning into their music.

The classic ideal, the abstract design of exquisite logic and a kind of dynamic-static balance, easily gave way. What Schubert had already begun, others—most of them still ignorant of the genius of their Viennese forbear—continued. The clear, rational outlines of the formal design became blurred. Harmony became richer, and composers willingly forgot the need to make sure that the crowd knew what key they were in, or where one movement ended and the next one began.

Schumann and Mendelssohn wrote symphonies in which one movement flowed into the next without pause, and in which music from one movement recurred in another. Instead of a balance of opposites, in other words, music began to assume a oneness, to be about something. Poking around in some forgotten Schubert, Franz Liszt found a marvelous fantasy for piano in which all four movements derived from a single theme that Schubert in his genius had continually transformed. Out of this model Liszt invented the symphonic poem. In France, meanwhile, Hector Berlioz began to create vast, outrageous symphonic panoramas in which the "subject matter" consisted of the fevered frustrations of his own life, a life that drew its motive power from one frustrated amour after the next.

Romanticism is a musical style of endless contradictions. It was the time of musical vastness: Berlioz, with his thousand performers in the *Grand Mass for the Dead*; Wagner with the immense tetralogy *The Ring of the Nibelungs*, in which all the arts unite in a twenty-hour retelling of the birth and death of mankind; Mahler with his vast neurotic symphonies. It was also the time of the perfect miniature: Chopin with the jeweled perfection of a ninety-second mazurka that could wring the heart; Schumann and, later, Hugo Wolf with songs often no more substantial than moonbeams.

Other elements also played their part. The 19th century was a time of nationalistic stirrings. Italy, under Garibaldi, finally did something for itself against the foreign powers that dominated parts of the land, and Verdi's operas rang with ill-concealed appeals to his countrymen's patriotism. German folk opera, from Weber's *Der Freischütz* through Wagner's

Ring and *Die Meistersinger*, instilled in Germans a sense of nationality that Bismarck came to crystallize. Longings for political freedom in the region now known as Czechoslovakia inspired splendid nationalistic music from Dvořák and Smetana. And, in Russia, groups of composers came together to throw off the yoke not of political domination, but of imported musical styles from the West to create an indigenous art.

And it was, above all, the time when all music finally took it upon itself, for better or for worse, to reach out toward an audience. The public virtuoso burst into the world's consciousness, abetted by a splendid knack for public relations. Niccolò Paganini made sure the story got around that his violin playing was the result of a one-to-one collaboration with the devil; Chopin swooned at the piano—in person or musically—and the ladies of Paris swooned in perfect tune. When Franz Liszt felt his public slipping away, he took holy orders and played again in full cloth. The great Swedish opera star, Jenny Lind, put herself, for her American appearances, into the hands of P. T. Barnum.

The virtuoso conductor also appeared on the scene, although not necessarily as clearly to the detriment of his music. Felix Mendelssohn enjoyed enormous popularity for himself and his elegant platform manner, but he was noble enough to use his prestige to plead the cause of music that might otherwise have gone unplayed. This extended all the way from Schubert's C-major Symphony (first played only in 1839, eleven years after its composer's death) to a large-scale revival, after nearly a century, of some of Johann Sebastian Bach's major works, including the *Passion According to St. Matthew*. Later there came Hans von Bülow, Hans Richter, and Liszt himself—all, apparently, men of impeccable training, of not always admirable selflessness, and all able to cope with the constant forward movement of musical horizons.

Romanticism was not, of course, a unanimity of style—anything but. It was, indeed, a time for heated emotion, which much of the music couldn't help but elicit. The era witnessed one more kind of show-biz phenomenon, the virtuoso critic. He was, first and foremost, Eduard Hanslick, early on a devoted admirer of Richard Wagner, later a virulent detractor—so much so that he achieved one kind of immortality when Wagner caricatured him as the pedant Beckmesser in *Die Meistersinger*. As a detractor of Wagner, Hanslick then had to be a supporter of Johannes Brahms and his music, as Brahms was set up as the avatar of all the conservative academic probity that Wagner stood against. That Brahms himself, of course, stood aloof from all this factionalism goes without saying. Very likely, however, even this saintly stick-in-the-mud realized that all the argle-bargle among supporters and detractors did, at least, sell a few more tickets. And so, of course, did Wagner.

Robert Schumann

b Zwickau, Saxony, June 8, 1810; *d* Endenich, near Bonn, July 29, 1856. Principal output includes: orchestral music (four symphonies; concertos for piano, violin, and cello; several concert overtures; short works for solo instruments and orchestra); chamber music (trios, quartets, and the well-known Quintet for Piano and Strings); piano music (three sonatas plus many collections of romantically named character pieces); the opera *Genoveva* and several dramatic cantatas based on literary sources; choral music both sacred and secular; and, above all, a vast reportoire of lieder to texts by the leading German poets of the day.

If the expressive poles of musical Romanticism were the grandiose and the intimate, Schumann clearly inclined toward the latter. His affinity for subtle mood painting and gentle lyricism found the ideal outlets in his marvelous song output (most of it composed in the throes of passion for Clara Wieck, the equally passionate composer-pianist, who did become his wife) and the closely related sets of small pieces for piano. Yet Schumann, besides being a composer, was also a literary figure, the leading critic for an influential music journal and an ardent, if self-proclaimed herald of the interaction between music's past and future. And as such, it surely seemed to him like some kind of debt to the mainstream of music to become, as well, a composer of orchestral works.

He never quite mastered the orchestra. There are moments in his Third (*Rhenish*) Symphony, the *Manfred* overture, and the Piano Concerto as inspired as any in music. But the long symphonic line did not come naturally to Schumann, nor did an insight into the way the orchestra could best honor his own inventions. His way of achieving momentum seems contrived, most of all because his own kind of long-breathed melody could not, from out of itself, supply the energy that a Beethoven melody possessed in explosive abundance. You sometimes get the feeling in a Schumann work for orchestra that, even though he has just stated a sublime idea, he is then treading water until the next idea comes along. The opening of the *Rhenish* is just such a case; in the first few minutes there seems to be nothing but climaxes, so much so that the music seems more exhausting than exalting.

Yet, the exuberant Romantic spirit in the music remains, and can be realized by a knowing performance. With its flaws, Schumann's orchestral music—the four symphonies most of all—signals the change in large-scale musical forms in the generations after Beethoven. No longer a grand, abstract design—which all Beethoven is, even when a title like *Pastoral* is furnished or a chorus brought in for a finale—the symphony now became a suggestive canvas, with a picture or a literary relationship brought to the fore. Two of the four symphonies, the *Rhenish* and the *Spring* are overtly pictorial, but this element is not lacking in their two unnamed fellows or in any of Schumann's other big orchestral scores. The soloist in the Piano Concerto, probably the least flawed of all Schumann's orchestral works, is clearly a Romantic protagonist, and his adventures can be taken down from the music almost as if by dictation.

SELECTED RECORDINGS

Symphonies Nos. 1–4
 –Rafael Kubelik and the Bavarian Symphony
 Orchestra (Columbia/CBS)
Symphony No. 1 in B-Flat Major
 –Otto Klemperer and the New Philharmonia
 Orchestra (Angel)
Symphony No. 3 in E flat *Rhenish*
 –Bruno Walter and the New York Philharmonic
 Orchestra (Columbia-Odyssey)
Symphony No. 4 in D minor
 –Wilhelm Furtwängler and the Berlin Philharmonic
 Orchestra (Deutsche Grammophon)
Piano Concerto in A minor
 –Arthur Rubinstein, soloist, with Carlo Maria
 Giulini and the Chicago Symphony Orchestra
 (RCA)
 –Myra Hess, soloist, with Rudolf Schwarz and the
 Philharmonia Orchestra (RCA)
 –Dinu Lipatti, soloist, with Herbert von Karajan
 and the Philharmonia Orchestra (Columbia)

Schumann's orchestral works do not play themselves;
they invite the conductor with great temperament but
also with the technique to balance the thickness in
Schumann's scoring that buries some of the music's
best ideas. Most conductors must tinker with the orchestration to make the music sound; the purists may
scream, but a performance "as the composer wrote it"'
in Schumann's case would deprive the world of some
splendid music.

Of the complete sets of the symphonies (four works
on three disks) Rafael Kubelik's version with the Bavarian Symphony beautifully underscores the marvelous lyricism in the music. Klemperer's complete
recording has its admirers, but the performances of the
Second and Third symphonies are vastly inferior in
strength to those of the First and Fourth. Two old but
vital performances, dating from the 1940s and, of
course, in monaural sound, are still worth hearing: the
amazingly vital Bruno Walter *Rhenish* and the intense
Furtwängler Fourth; these are performances that be-

long to a philosophical mainstream extending back to Schumann himself.

Rubinstein's splendid realization of the tenderness and splendor of the near-perfect Piano Concerto is just about ideal, yet there is a kind of poetry in each of two distinctive versions from the past—those of Myra Hess and of Dinu Lipatti—that will reward a search.

Felix Mendelssohn

b **Hamburg, February 3, 1809; *d* Leipzig, November 4, 1847. Principal output includes: five symphonies; two piano concertos and one violin concerto (plus several youthful concertos and twelve symphonies for strings); several concert overtures; incidental music to Shakespeare's *A Midsummer Night's Dream*; a large output of chamber music, including an octet for strings sometimes orchestrally performed; piano music, notably the large collection called *Songs Without Words*; two operas; two oratorios; and considerable religious and secular choral music, songs, and organ works.**

Grandson of Moses Mendelssohn, one of the foremost Jewish philosophers of all time, the young Felix found his way among musicians made easier when, at the age of 17, he underwent baptism. Even so, his early days in Hamburg were filled with acrimony; it was difficult for hardworking musicians to accept the easy charm of a mere boy who, at 18, had composed the marvelous overture to *A Midsummer Night's Dream* and the buoyant Octet for Strings. Not until he was 20, when he accomplished a feat that was beyond challenge, did Mendelssohn win the respect of his hometown.

That feat was the revival of Bach's *Passion According to St. Matthew*, music known for over a century only by name. It is likely, from accounts, that the revival was in a drastically truncated and altered form, yet the effect upon the musical world was in the nature of a revelation, and the musical acumen of Mendelssohn was praised by all.

It was, perhaps, prophetic of Mendelssohn's own music that his reputation should have been made by the revival of music by a man regarded as conservative in his own time. Mendelssohn himself embodied a curious but workable mixture of adventurer and conservative. Against the exuberant onrush of Schumann, the Mendelssohn genre seems like classic repose. His symphonies, especially the best-known Third (the *Scotch*) and Fourth (the *Italian*), have, along with their ever-so-slight pictorialism, a sense of returning to the clarity of bygone classic models. There is an earnestness about them, as in the finely oratorical epilogue to the *Scotch*, but the music is also marked by elegance and immense clarity.

The best of Mendelssohn's orchestral writing is his impeccable sense of brightly lit tone color. The elfin, delicate fairyland evocation at the start of the *Midsummer Night's Dream* overture is a Mendelssohn trademark that is unmistakably his even when imitated by others (as in Gilbert and Sullivan's fairy music for *Iolanthe*). It shows up again even in non-elfin context, as in the scherzo of the *Scotch*, and it irradiates the piano writing in the two brief concertos and in the magical finale of the Violin Concerto.

The Violin Concerto is, beyond doubt, Mendelssohn's most satisfactory orchestral composition. Its melodic prodigality is astonishing. It is written with enormous regard for the soloist as both virtuoso and artistic statesman. The elegance of its craftsmanship is a world of delight in itself; note particularly, in the last movement, the splendid way new countermelodies occur in the orchestra above or below the violinist's principal theme. The concerto is one of the few works whose every secret comes forward on first hearing, yet whose power to delight never cloys on repetition.

His sojourns in England, where he was beloved as a native musician (by a country that has had few), resulted in a turning in his style toward a correct, if rather bloodless mode of expression much to the Victorian taste. (Since this turn resulted in relatively little orchestral music, that deploration will be continued in a subsequent volume.) An earlier English (and Scottish) jaunt did give us the concert overture *The Hebrides* (or "Fingal's Cave"), a splendid piece of orchestral depiction, quite the most purely romantic of Mendelssohn's creations for orchestra.

SELECTED RECORDINGS

Symphonies No. 3 in A minor, No. 4 in A major and No. 5 in D major
–Claudio Abbado and the London Symphony Orchestra (London/Decca)

Symphonies No. 3 and No. 4
– Riccardo Muti and the New Philharmonia Orchestra (Angel)

Symphonies No. 4 in A major and No. 5 in D major
–Raymond Leppard and the English Chamber Orchestra (RCA)

Violin Concerto in E minor
–Nathan Milstein, violinist, with Claudio Abbado and the Vienna Philharmonic Orchestra (Deutsche Grammophon)
–Joseph Szigeti, violinist, with Sir Thomas Beecham and the London Philharmonic Orchestra (Columbia)

A Midsummer Night's Dream, incidental music
–soloists and chorus, with Bernard Haitink and the Amsterdam Concertgebouw Orchestra (Philips)

There is little enough Italian in the *Italian* symphony to justify the performances by Abbado and Muti on those grounds; it's just that both young conductors have the command over orchestral sonority and the liveliness of spirit to make Mendelssohn's music work. Even so, there is a special quality in the Leppard recording of the *Italian* (along with the less interesting No. 5, the so-called *Reformation* symphony). The performances use a chamber orchestra, and Mendelssohn's radiant scoring for winds stands out as in no other performance.

Milstein's sturdy way with the Violin Concerto has been a matter of public knowledge for nearly half a century, and the veteran violinist still knows all the music's secrets. But so, to an even greater extent, did the noble Hungarian violinist Joseph Szigeti, in the miraculous collaboration with Beecham that was recorded in the mid-1930s. It is currently available only in a six-record Szigeti collection—every note of which, however, is to be treasured.

The *Midsummer Night's Dream* music is, to most people, the quintessence of "Mendelssohnianism"—meaning not only the elfin shimmer of the opening of the overture and the whole of the scherzo, but also the shapely, elegant "prettiness" of the nocturne. The wonder is not only that Mendelssohn could write such music as the overture in his teens, but also that he could return, years later, and recapture the same tone for the later sections. Haitink's performance, which includes the brief vocal sections (marvelous on their own), has the wisdom we associate with his work, and the orchestra's playing is a miracle in itself.

Hector Berlioz

b La Cote-St.-André, France, December 11, 1803; *d* Paris, March 8, 1869. Principal output includes: two symphonies *(Symphonie Fantastique* and *Harold in Italy)*; six concert overtures and several short pieces (plus orchestral passages from vocal and choral works that have achieved independent concert life); three operas; several major choral works defying exact categorization (the "dramatic symphony" *Roméo et Juliette*, the cantata *La Damnation de Faust*, the oratorio *L'Enfance du Christ*); a Te Deum, a *Grande Messe des Morts* (Requiem), and shorter works; and songs and vocal ensembles with piano and with orchestra.

If the mere listing of Berlioz's music runs into snags of definition, such is also the key to his artistry as a whole. No prominent musician ever came to his craft so inadequately trained. Berlioz never mastered an instrument, and his belligerence toward any teacher who tried to implant a sense of rules met with scorn. His sets of Memoirs, still in print, are probably the most colorful account ever written of artistic paranoia.

Fortunately, Berlioz was constantly able to harness his own mental hangups and use them as motive power for his incredibly adventurous music. His *Symphonie Fantastique*, composed in 1830 while Beethoven was barely cold in his grave, is pure musical psychosis; its program explains that its five movements represent the dreams of someone who, in despond over unrequited love, has overdosed on drugs. Berlioz wrote it while despondent over unrequited love for a visiting English actress, Harriet Smithson, who had no inkling at the time of Berlioz's existence. (Many years later they did meet and marry, to the intense boredom of both.)

From its misty opening to the diabolical orchestral howls in the concluding "Witches Sabbath," this symphony proposes a use of music, and of the orchestra, that strides precipitously into a new era. There are virtuoso effects that have become famous: the fearful chords of kettledrums in the movement depicting the "loved one" when it (she) appears during the witches' revels, the passages in this finale where violins tap the wooden frame of their bows on the strings, thus creating the dancing of skeletons. But actually every note of the symphony has something new—be it marvelous or exasperating. Right at the beginning, the way the violins touch the top note of those rising arpeggios sounds the way distant lights look. The waltz in the ensuing "Ballroom Scene" is delectably scored, the two harps so delicate as to be almost unheard. And the pastoral third movement, ending with two shepherds piping at one another from off in the distance, with thunder rolling almost imperceptibly in the farther distance—surely nothing like this had entered music before!

Everything out of Berlioz's flaming imagination created some kind of effect; the wonder is that so much of it is truly, hauntingly beautiful besides. His sense of melody is light years apart from the clear, symmetrical phrasing of Beethoven and Schubert. The tune for solo viola in the symphony *Harold in Italy* (based, from a very great distance, on the character created by Lord Byron) is a single, unbroken arch of melody that leaves the hearer breathless just by following it. The overt appeal of the loud and evil side of Berlioz is undeniable—and this must include the depiction of Judgment Day in the Requiem for which four choruses, four brass ensembles, and four pairs of timpani players land on the same note at the same time, not to mention the "Ride to Hades" at the end of the *Damnation of Faust.*

But the exquisite, delicate side of his music lingers even longer in the memory: the minuet and Sylphs' Dance from the *Damnation*, in which the impalpable area just this side of silence is orchestrated in myriad ways; the ravishing orchestral passage in the choral symphony in *Romeo and Juliet* depicting the lovers' one night together with a poignancy beyond even Shakespeare's own words; the whole of the oratorio on *L'Enfance du Christ*, all of it scored for the most delicate of performing forces, so reserved and exquisite that Berlioz was able to pass it off for years as an anonymous work from a bygone era. That, of course, strikes us as sheer nonsense; only the strange, tortured, exultant Berlioz could have written a note of this or any other of his scores. His music seems to have been born within his head with virtually no relation to any artistic past; no composer since his time even tried to carry on from where he left off.

SELECTED RECORDINGS

Symphonie Fantastique
—Colin Davis and the Amsterdam Concertgebouw Orchestra (Philips)
—Pierre Boulez and the London Symphony Orchestra (Columbia)

Harold in Italy
—Yehudi Menuhin, solo viola, with Colin Davis and the Philharmonia Orchestra (Angel/HMV)

Roméo et Juliette
—Soloists and chorus with Colin Davis and the London Symphony Orchestra (Philips)
—Orchestral excerpts only; Carlo Maria Giulini and the Chicago Symphony Orchestra (Philips)
—Pierre Boulez and the New York Philharmonic (Columbia)

In a great British tradition that embraces such past masters as Sir Thomas Beecham and Sir Hamilton Harty, Colin Davis has become known as the sovereign interpreter of Berlioz in our time. His own lively, and, at the same time, careful, sense of rhythm stands him in good stead here, especially when a Berlioz melody seems to arch toward infinity in defiance of gravity. But above all, Davis's marvelous orchestral ear, his ability to balance not only the smashing effects at climactic points but also the extraordinary delicate moments (such as the shepherds' dialogue in the *Fantastique* described above) make him a spectacular exponent of this music.

Pierre Boulez has also conducted some marvelous Berlioz performances; his own extraordinary command over orchestral tone seems to lay bare the most complex sonority and to let air flow through some very dense music. His performances tend to be somewhat dry as compared to those by Davis, but there is no question of his love and respect for his extraordinary countryman's music. Acquire the complete *Roméo* if you possibly can (it runs to two disks); some of the vocal music, including the mezzo-soprano's first invocation to Shakespeare, is most haunting. For the familiar orchestral excerpts, Giulini's Chicago performance is noble and probing.

Franz Liszt

b Raiding, Hungary, October 22, 1811; *d* Bayreuth, July 31, 1886. Principal output includes: for orchestra—two symphonies (*Faust* and *Dante*), twelve symphonic poems, two piano concertos, and other works (such as *Totentanz, Malediction,* and *Hungarian Fantasy*); for piano and orchestra— *Mephisto Waltz* and miscellaneous short works; masses, oratorios, and numerous shorter choral works; a vast quantity of piano music; and some chamber works and many songs.

In person he was Romanticism embodied: the mystical presence, topped with the ascetic features and the flowing mane, the diabolical skill at the piano and on the podium, the affectations that went all the way from an insistence on speaking French (even in his native Hungary, whose own language he chose not to master) to a brilliant gift for self-exploitation even when clad in the vestments of the abbé he later became.

Yet Liszt was no fly-by-night charlatan; along with his flamboyance and his catalogue of *amours impropres* (which included the famous and versatile courtesan Lola Montez), Liszt was one of the true creative geniuses of his time, an innovator and an ardent champion of innovation in others. He conducted large-scale works of Berlioz throughout Europe when everyone else feared to touch the Frenchman's music; he nearly gave up his own music to apply himself to the cause of Richard Wagner (as a reward for which Wagner made off with Liszt's daughter Cosima, despite her being married to another).

Liszt's greatest fame was as a pianist, playing his own or others' music. He used the piano as none had before, and proposed that the instrument could reproduce any effect that the orchestra could. Yet, he also wrote brilliantly for orchestra and, while he made numerous piano transcriptions of other people's orchestral scores, he created relatively few of his own works. His orchestration was like everything else about him: brilliant, somewhat garish, larger than life. The conductor who doesn't land like an atomic bomb on the brass scoring in the peroration to *Les préludes* hasn't begun to understand the music.

Les préludes is one of a set of twelve works for which Liszt invented the term "symphonic poem." The title suggests the core of the Romantic ideal: a music that isn't merely artistic design, but also embodies poetry or painting or both into a singleness of expression. Liszt admittedly drew his inspiration for the technique in these works from the famous *Wanderer* fantasy for piano by Franz Schubert, one of the few of his works known at all well at the time. In Schubert's four-movement work, a single theme, taken from a song called "The Wanderer," undergoes transformation to serve as contrasting bases for all four connected movements. Liszt turned Schubert's music into a piano concerto, and took its outline as his own guide. In most of the symphonic poems, and even in longer works like the hour-long symphonies inspired by Goethe's *Faust* and by Dante's *Divine Comedy*, the themes stated at the outset behave like characters in a drama. They grow or diminish, they change in character; they are wavering and fragile one moment, but return decked out in full orchestral finery the next.

In most of these symphonic poems you may detect the remnant of the old-fashioned symphonic plan of separate movements. Beethoven (in his Fifth and Sixth symphonies) had already begun to run movements together without pause, breaking down the clear contrast so prized by the classicists; Mendelssohn and Schumann had also run movements together in most of their symphonies. Now Liszt created a continuous musical structure with sections in different tempos, but with no breaks at all. The notion of a singleness—of mood or of artistic purpose—is one of the Romantic ideals, carried to its extreme connotation in the twenty-odd hours of Wagner's *Ring of the Nibelungs.* It also played a major role in Liszt's musical thinking.

SELECTED RECORDINGS

A *Faust* Symphony; *Les préludes*
  –Leonard Bernstein and the New York Philharmonic Orchestra, with men's chorus in the finale of the symphony (Columbia)
Three Symphonic Poems: *Mazeppa, Orpheus, Battle of the Huns*
  –Zubin Mehta and the Los Angeles Philharmonic (London/Decca)
Piano Concertos Nos. 1 and 2
  –Sviatoslav Richter, pianist, with Kiril Kondrashin and the London Philharmonic Orchestra (Philips)

Wanderer Fantasy; *Totentanz*
  —Alfred Brendel, pianist, with Michael Gielen and
  the Vienna Volksoper Orchestra (Turnabout)

It isn't exactly necessary to be Liszt to conduct Liszt, but it can help, which is why the flamboyance of Leonard Bernstein and Zubin Mehta, the Lisztian panache with which they conduct their own lives on or off the stage, turns them into sensationally good conductors of their spiritual ancestor. There is a breadth and dazzlement in Bernstein's conducting of the spacious (if somewhat repetitive) three-movement symphony on *Faust* (which could be taken as three interlinked symphonic poems) that fairly leaps off the record. Mehta's recording is of three lesser known poems, of which the quiet, poetic *Orpheus* may rise higher in your affections than its gaudy fellows; again, he seems ideally suited for this music (as he is, alas, for little else).

The two piano concertos are early works, each in several connected movements and each making use of the process of thematic transformation as do the symphonies and symphonic poems. Again, amid all the recordings that concentrate on the external flashiness in this music (of which there is considerable), Richter's performance seems to bask in a more inventive kind of exuberance, as if he were taking part in the creation of the music. The two other concerted works are played by Brendel with honorable scholarship, if some reticence, but there is no competing version of the fascinating *Wanderer*, the work based on Schubert's composition for solo piano.

Richard Wagner

b Leipzig, May 22, 1813; *d* Venice, February 13, 1883. Principal output includes: orchestral music (a youthful symphony, several short pieces for band or orchestra, including *Festival March* for the Philadelphia Centennial Exposition in 1876, a *Faust* overture, and the *Siegfried Idyll*); some choral works (including *The Apostles' Last Supper*); piano and chamber music of no great consequence; many

songs, including the five songs to texts of Mathilde Wesendonck; and, above all, thirteen music dramas out of which an orchestral repertoire can be drawn.

Richard Wagner was the nastiest great composer who has ever lived. Ruthless, supremely arrogant, incapable of honoring personal loyalties, he saw the world as composed exclusively of Wagnerites and anti-Wagnerites—the latter beneath contempt, the former to be manipulated at whim. The world owed him an extravagant living, he decided, and he lived to collect that debt. His life was that of the quintessential Romantic and, at the same time, the most grotesque exaggeration of the Romantic notion of the artist as hero, savior, raison d'etre for all humanity.

He came late to music, after feverishly assimilating the literature and music of his past, particularly those elements that could establish the supremacy of a pure German art—including Beethoven's *Fidelio* and Weber's *Der Freischütz*. After three youthful operas, at best imitations of lesser Romantic models, he embarked on his own course with *The Flying Dutchman, Tannhäuser,* and *Lohengrin.* Embodied in them, and even more in the masterpieces to follow—*Tristan und Isolde, Die Meistersinger,* the *Ring of the Nibelungen* tetralogy, and *Parsifal*—was an infinitely bold, original synthesis of music, poetry, drama, and the visual arts, blended into what he called the "total art-work."

Musically, the Wagnerian music drama was like nothing before it: a continuous flow of melody, no longer honoring the separation into recitative and aria and, in the late works, no longer honoring the classic necessity of coming to cadence in some predetermined and clearly defined key. The orchestra, no longer merely a support for the singers, often actually bore the major dramatic substance, an interweaving of musical motives that defined both character and concept in the drama. Frequently, the singer's voice is like an afterthought—an additional line over a self-sufficient orchestral drama. This aspect of Wagner's music legitimizes, to some extent, at least, the extraction of sections from his dramas to be performed as orchestral compositions, with or even without singers.

From the first note of *Tristan und Isolde* a vision of the universe unfolds—dark, brooding, tortuously chromatic to illuminate from within the torment of unfulfilled passion until the final release through death. In *Die Meistersinger* there is something quite the opposite, an ardent and romantic comedy, set in Renaissance Germany but peopled by recognizable types—among them at least one unmistakable anti-Wagnerian, none other than the music critic Eduard Hanslick, a.k.a. Beckmesser.

In the massive cycle of *The Ring* Wagner embodied his obsession with German mythology; in four evenings of performance one is confronted with the history of an entire race and thus of all mankind, encircled by a devastating parable on the corruption of power. And at the end of Wagner's life there is *Parsifal*, a final surprise from the obscene blasphemer, a consecration play on the mystery of Redemption: music drama as religious service.

It is impossible to overstate the breadth and depth of Wagner's achievement, or the emotional impact, bordering on ecstasy, that his music can instill in the listener. No composer before or since created so stupendous a body of sheer artistic daring. Wagner, born to conquer, throttled the musical world with conceptions too vast for comprehension.

Nearly a century after his death, Wagner's influence cannot be fully assessed. The countless superficial attempts to imitate the scale, if not the substance, of his music dramas can well be forgotten, but the emanations from his musical innovations, the horizons he revealed or merely hinted at, are still in evidence. His concept of the leitmotif—the musical embodiment of a character or idea that can then be manipulated to undergo psychological change—and his implied challenge to the concept of a tonal centrality that had served composers since the Baroque, changed the subsequent course of music. Without these, the musical line that runs from Wagner through Mahler to Schoenberg to Webern and to the wildest musical frontiers would have followed a vastly different course. The man who could prophesy the twilight of the gods may also have prophesied the twilight of music, or so some like to surmise.

Whether or not that is true, there is one further matter to consider with Wagner. The very controversialism of his music gave rise to something hitherto unknown: the rise of a musical cult, and the sealing off of one segment of the musical public from the rest of the world through a wall of intellectualism. The seriousness of purpose—the mysticism, even—that Wagner and the Wagnerites invoked was in some ways the beginning of self-conscious connoisseurship, the divisions in music between "serious" and "popular," the infusion of a sense of the arcane into concert- and opera-going. We still live under that shadow today, even though the relationship that Wagner himself ordained between artist and society has collapsed before our eyes in this century with the thud of Valhalla.

SELECTED RECORDINGS

Siegfried Idyll; Tannhäuser Overture and Venusberg Music; *Lohengrin* Prelude
   –Bruno Walter and the Columbia Symphony Orchestra (Columbia)
Excerpts from *The Ring of the Nibelungen*
   –George Szell and the Cleveland Orchestra (Columbia)
Excerpts from various music dramas
   –Otto Klemperer and the Philharmonia Orchestra (Angel)
Siegfried Idyll; Preludes: *Lohengrin, Parsifal,* and *Tristan und Isolde;* "Ride of the Valkyries" from *Die Walküre*
   –Wilhelm Furtwängler and the Vienna Philharmonic Orchestra (two-record set) (Angel-Seraphim)
Parsifal excerpts, etc.
   –Bruno Walter and the Columbia Symphony Orchestra (Columbia)

To understand Wagner fully, one must be prepared to go to the opera house or, at least, to devote five hours to listening to one of the complete music dramas on records. To experience a series of selections from these complete works, especially on a recording that juxtaposes selections from different dramas, is to skim only the surface power that the music has in context. Yet, so great is the power of Wagner's own thinking, and so sure his own sense of orchestration, that even short excerpts can, in the right hands, make their point. And when all else fails, there is the one self-sufficient work from Wagner's maturity, the divinely beautiful *Siegfried Idyll* (composed as a Christmas present to Wagner's ill-gotten wife Cosima after the birth of their son Siegfried), an artful interweaving of some of the more tender musical motives from *The Ring* (plus one honest-to-god folksong).

The earliest master of Wagnerian style to be documented on record (although in monaural) is the great Wilhelm Furtwängler, whose performances have an incandescence, a natural and spontaneous ebb and flow, and an emotional intimacy not since equaled.

Of the conductors recorded in stereo, Klemperer and Walter bring to the music ripe maturity and a warm Romantic glow. Especially noteworthy is Walter's incomparable performance of the Paris version of *Tannhäuser*'s opening music, which contains astonishing harmonic flights of fancy remarkable in this opera of Wagner's comparative youth.

The Szell performance is also the most satisfying available representation of the orchestral interludes from *The Ring*. As is often done, Szell tacks the closing pages of the entire cycle on to the end of Siegfried's Funeral Music (which occurs a half-hour earlier); by such surgery must an orchestral repertoire be assembled. Finally, Walter's recording of the prelude and "Good Friday Spell" from *Parsifal* should be required listening, for the serenity of the late Wagner and its realization by the late Walter. This is the music that melted the heart of Claude Debussy, one of the most resolute of anti-Wagnerians.

Johannes Brahms

b **Hamburg, May 7, 1833;** *d* **Vienna, April 3, 1897. Principal output includes: orchestral works (four symphonies, four concertos—two for piano, one for violin, and one for violin and cello—two serenades for small orchestra, and two concert overtures); chamber music (sonatas, trios, quartets, quintets,**

and sextets for various combinations); music for piano solo; choral music (the *German Requiem* and several shorter works); and a great many songs, including arrangements of German folksongs.

The musical world in the mid-19th century, at least the German- and English-speaking segments, was virtually divided between supporters of Brahms, the conservative who sought to rekindle in music the spirit of classicism, and the supporters of Richard Wagner, the revolutionary with fantastic notions of the "total art-work" and of a future with himself at approximately the center. The schism was in large part a media event, fanned by partisan disciples (we'd call them "groupies" today) and especially by the anti-Wagnerian critic Eduard Hanslick. In the heat of battle some of the combatants may have forgotten which side they were on; Clara Schumann, Brahms' closest friend, found his First Symphony lacking in melody, and Hanslick declared that it lacked invention.

For admirer and detractor alike, the melody and invention in Brahms' music should be beyond argument. No more warm-hearted melodist existed than the man who wrote the waltzlike second theme in the first movement of the Second Symphony (or the immortal "Cradle Song" that it resembles), the finale of the Second Piano Concerto, or the slow scherzo of the Third Symphony. As for invention, Brahms may indeed have possessed too much for his own good. His studies of Beethoven gave him the discipline to mold recalcitrant musical materials into logical, eloquent structures; there is a diabolical manipulativeness in Brahms' typical large-scale works—the way, for example, tiny fragments of inner voices in the orchestra introduction to the Violin Concerto, seemingly insignificant at first, later surface as full-blooded melodies. There is so much going on at any moment in his music that his orchestral textures at times become restless and thick.

There has always been, and probably always will

be, a certain critical reservation about Brahms—that his nostalgia for "classic perfection" could lead him toward academicism. It is true that his symphonies lack the spontaneity of classic masterpieces. His musical style is often overshadowed by just a touch of stodgy, Victorian sentimentality; this, plus a conscious striving to achieve the definitive greatness, can make the music wearisome at times. The least burdensome of his orchestral music is probably the Second Piano Concerto, in which the beautifully conceived solo part comes through the orchestra like a beacon.

Yet, the warmheartedness of all of Brahms' best music deserves all the acclaim it is usually accorded. A passion for Brahms does seem to come and go among audiences. He may at times have overcompensated for the exuberance of other Romantic composers by burdening his music with an excess of learnedness, but Brahms is never dry or bitter, and the oratorical eloquence of his best music is lit with the warmth of his own humanism.

SELECTED RECORDINGS

Symphonies Nos. 1–4 (plus the Academic Festival and Tragic Overtures and the Variations on a Theme by Haydn)
   –Bruno Walter and the Columbia Symphony Orchestra (four separate records) (Columbia)
Symphony No. 1 in C minor
   –Otto Klemperer and the Philharmonia Orchestra (Angel/HMV)
   –Wilhelm Furtwängler and the Vienna Philharmonic Orchestra (EMI)
Symphony No. 2 in D major
   –Pierre Monteux and the London Symphony Orchestra (London/Philips)
Symphonies No. 3 in F major and No. 4 in E minor
   –Carlo Maria Giulini and the Philharmonia Orchestra (No. 3) and the Chicago Symphony Orchestra (No. 4) (Angel)
Piano Concertos No. 1 in D minor and No. 2 in B-flat major
   –Rudolf Serkin, soloist, with George Szell and the Cleveland Orchestra (two separate records or two-record set) (Columbia)

Violin Concerto in D major
–David Oistrakh, soloist, with Otto Klemperer and the French National Radio Symphony Orchestra (Angel/EMI)

Serenades No. 1 in D major and No. 2 in A major
–Istvan Kertesz and the London Symphony Orchestra (London/Decca)

Like that of all Romantics, Brahms' music is founded on rich, luxuriant harmonies and robust, eloquent melodic lines. These elements, combined with the contrapuntal activity in his textures, can make his music seem thick. The challenge to the conductor, therefore, is to take care that the musical line remains unclogged. Bruno Walter had this gift, and the recordings he made in his eighties are remarkably youthful documents. Klemperer's Brahms tends to be weightier, but the profundity of his approach is unmistakable. The visionary Furtwängler performance (in monaural only, of course) of No. 1, Pierre Monteux's leisurely performance of No. 2 (the most leisurely of the symphonies), and the broad, flexible Giulini performances of the last two symphonies are also worth considering.

Serkin's fiery performances of the two piano concertos are aided greatly by George Szell's marvelous orchestral control. Of the many performances of the Violin Concerto, none captures the wild intensity of the piece, especially its gypsylike finale, better than the late Oistrakh in his collaboration with Klemperer. And the two delightful serenades—light-textured works for people who think they don't like Brahms, as well as for those who think they do—are nicely served in the splendid Istvan Kertesz performances.

CZECHOSLOVAK NATIONALISM

Antonin Dvořák
b **Nelahozeves, near Prague, September 8, 1841;**
d **Prague, May 1, 1904**

Bedřich Smetana
b **Litomysl, March 2, 1824;**
d **Prague, May 12, 1884**

Principal output includes: orchestral works, nine symphonies by Dvořák, and three concertos (piano, violin, cello) by Dvořák; and symphonic poems and concert overtures by both, including cycles (*Nature, Life* and *Love* by Dvořák; *My Country* by Smetana). Also: by both composers, numerous operas dealing with both nationalistic and Romantic subjects; choral works; chamber works, including quartets and trios; and piano music and songs.

Bedřich Smetana

Europe was swept throughout the 19th century by a desire to assert national belonging, and to express this through art that drew on the folkways of a country. The reasons for this nationalistic movement were manifold. Politics certainly played a part. Poland, Italy, and the lands on the outer reaches of the unstable Austrian Empire were particularly anxious to throw off the burden of foreign rule and reassert their own personalities in their own languages. But there were artistic reasons as well. There had been a certain homogeneity in the musical language from Paris and London in the west to St. Petersburg in the east; the German classics were played by all orchestras, and the Italian operas sung by all opera companies in Europe.

To this growing sense of national identity, musicians contributed considerably. In Italy, the early operas of Verdi were loaded with analogies to that country's political state of affairs, a fact soon spotted by ardent nationalists who even took Verdi's own name as an acronym for their struggle to restore the Italian monarchy (*Vittorio Emmanuele Re Degli Italiani*). And in Bohemia, two major composers of a somewhat less bellicose frame of mind applied themselves to two ideas: Smetana and Dvořák wanted to become internationally successful as composers and to use their music to spread throughout the world the beauties and lore of their native Bohemia.

Smetana was the older, and the first to achieve recognition. This came about partly through his brilliant operas—*Dalibor*, a broad historical pageant of a bygone Bohemian freedom fighter, and *The Bartered Bride*, a delicious folk comedy whose dances were infused with national flavor. But Smetana's message was also carried in his orchestral masterpiece, a set of six interrelated symphonic poems called *Ma Vlast* (My Country). The six are interrelated in the fact that certain themes, which the composer wants us to identify with certain pictorial elements, recur from one work to the next. Thus, the poem called *The High Castle* describes a noble edifice at the mouth of the Moldau, and when, in the poem called *The Moldau*, the river reaches its broadest expanse, the "High Castle" theme is again heard. The works themselves are planned somewhat along Lisztian lines of thematic transformation, yet virtually all the material has the flavor of folksong and dance.

Antonin Dvořák

Dvořák's career lasted longer, and he moved more freely than his older countryman in international musical circles. Johannes Brahms took an interest in his work, and helped his younger colleague to gain access to publishers. There is, to be sure, a Brahmsian stamp on some of Dvořák's symphonic work, but not to its disadvantage. In what is widely regarded as the most profound of the symphonies, No. 7 in D minor, there is a Brahmsian somberness and massiveness in the first and last movements; yet Dvořák's own melodic sense flowed more freely than that of Brahms, and the exuberance that makes his music move, and the almost childlike love of its own beauty that surges through his work, are qualities that Brahms seemed too reserved to aspire to in his own work.

Almost all of Dvořák's music has some trait that bespeaks his land of origin. Several of the symphonies (notably Nos. 6, 7 and—despite its title *New World*—No. 9) have scherzo movements unmistakably Czechoslovakian in their rhythms. Only No. 8, written for a London musical society, seems at home in the international German symphonic mainstream.

It is well known that Dvořák came to the United States and taught there for some years, while creating some of his most popular and profound masterworks, including the *New World* symphony and the Cello Concerto. The former may, or may not, contain American tunes Dvořák may have discovered in New York. The Cello Concerto has not a trace; it is simply an extraordinarily eloquent work, gorgeously written for its soloist, by a composer of broad horizons. These two works, because of their American origin, have long been the most popular of Dvořák's orchestral works, as the so-called *American Quartet* has been among his chamber works.

Recent years, however, have seen Dvořák's full splendor restored to concert life through the earlier published symphonies, as well as four splendid youthful symphonies, charming if somewhat overlaid with other people's musical influences, that were not published in Dvořák's lifetime. A rather striking number of modern conductors play Dvořák well; dull-witted indeed is the cellist who fails to draw inspiration from the wondrous concerto. The repertoire of short pieces—among them several symphonic poems and such endearing dance-inspired pieces as the *Scherzo Capriccioso* and the three *Slavonic Rhapsodies*—have also been dusted off in the past few years and found worthy. Once regarded as a minor Brahms, Dvořák's reputation has so grown through familiarity with his music that the comparison may conceivably be reversed some day.

SELECTED RECORDINGS

Smetana
My Country (complete cycle)
    –Raphael Kubelik and the Vienna Philharmonic
    Orchestra (London/Decca)
The Moldau (only);
    –George Szell and the Cleveland Orchestra
    (Columbia-Odyssey)

Dvořák
Complete Symphonies
    –Raphael Kubelik and the Berlin Philharmonic
    Orchestra (Deutsche Grammophon)

Symphony No. 5 in F major
–Raphael Kubelik and the Berlin Philharmonic
Orchestra (Deutsche Grammophon)
Symphony No. 6 in D major
–Istvan Kertesz and the London Symphony
Orchestra (London/Decca)
Symphony No. 7 in D minor
–Carlo Maria Giulini and the London Philharmonic
Orchestra (Angel)
Symphony No. 8 in G major
–Carlo Maria Giulini and the Chicago Symphony
Orchestra (Deutsche Grammophon)
Symphony No. 9 in E Minor *(New World)*
–George Szell and the Cleveland Orchestra
(Columbia)
–Carlo Maria Giulini and the Chicago Symphony
Orchestra (Deutsche Grammophon)
Cello Concerto in B minor
–Mstislav Rostropovitch, cellist, with Carlo Maria
Giulini and the London Philharmonic Orchestra
(Angel)
–Pablo Casals, cellist, with George Szell and the
Czech Philharmonic Orchestra (Seraphim/EMI)

It is perhaps understandable that the best recordings
of Bohemian music should be conducted by men from
that region, and, indeed, the Czech-born Kubelik and
the Hungarians Szell and Kertesz are all marvelously
sympathetic to the broad expanse of this music and
have the patience to allow the music to expand in its
own easygoing style. But the eloquence that the Italian
Giulini brings to this music is extraordinary, and there
is reason to favor his recordings over the considerable
competition for a nobility and a musical clarity that
are almost unique on records. Perhaps it is the nature
of Dvořák—his warmth of emotion is so readily accessible—to inspire this kind of performance, because
there is also the legendary Casals performance of the
Cello Concerto, recorded in prewar Prague long before
the conductor, George Szell, was known outside central Europe, that ranks on most people's list as one of
the greatest performance of anything on records. Not
that the broad, eloquent Rostropovitch-Giulini is so

poor an alternative, should the primitive sound of the Casals—or its occasional disappearance from circulation—put you off. Dvorak's Cello Concerto, simply as music, is one of the art's few imperatives, a work virtually impossible not to love.

THE RUSSIAN "FIVE"

Mily Balakirev
b Nizhny-Novgorod, January 2, 1837;
d St. Petersburg, May 29, 1910

César Cui
b Vilno, January 18, 1835;
d St. Petersburg, 24, 1918

Alexander Borodin
b St. Petersburg, November 12, 1833;
d St. Petersburg, February 27, 1887

Modest Mussorgsky
b Karevo, Pskov, March 21, 1839;
d St. Petersburg, March 28, 1887

Nicholas Rimsky-Korsakov
b Tikhivin, Novgorod, March 18, 1844;
d St. Petersburg, June 21, 1908

Principal output includes: orchestral music: suites (Rimsky- Korsakov's *Sheherazade* and several from his operas, four by Cui); symphonies (three by Borodin, one by Balakirev, three by Rimsky-Korsakov); symphonic poems (several by all composers); and concert overtures (several by all composers). Also: piano music by all composers, major operas on nationalistic themes by all composers (also, by Rimsky-Korsakov, several on Oriental subjects); and choral music, including settings of Russian liturgy, by all composers.

Modest Mussorgsky

Nowhere in Europe was the obsession greater to establish a national artistic expression than in czarist Russia; indeed, some of the edicts issued by the more militant of the Romantic-era artists sound suspiciously like some of the restrictive declarations by the Soviets on the way art should serve its nation. Be that as it may, five composers more or less threw their lots in with one another to establish Russia as a nation with its own musical expression. They had far to go.

Russia, by the 1870s, was a cosmopolitan center for the arts. St. Petersburg, the cultural capital, saw the major creators of Europe come and go; even the great Verdi wrote his *La Forza del Destino* for its opera house. Mikhail Glinka (1804–57) had already written major operas on Russian subjects (*A Life for the Tsar*, *Russlan and Ludmilla*), but the most ardent nationalists were quick to spot in this music the evidence that Glinka had perfected his style while studying in the opera houses of Italy; he stood, therefore, as both pioneer and traitor.

The force behind the formation of the "Five" was Mily Balakirev, the one member of the group with what could pass for professional musical training. The lack of conservatory training among the others—Borodin, in fact, was a chemist with some worldwide renown—was not entirely a hindrance to their ideals; it forced them, in fact, to fall back for material on what they knew best, namely, folksong and dance.

Mily Balakirev

Balakirev showed the way, with his piano work (later orchestrated) called *Islamey*, in which folk elements appeared. Borodin's best works, some created during his studies with Balakirev, seldom quote actual folk music; the composer assimilated the folk style and then wrote his own music within its bounds. Thus, his splendid Second

Symphony, unmistakably Russian in mood, contains little or no actual traditional material. Mussorgsky's masterpiece, the opera *Boris Godunov*, does use folk themes here and there, but the orchestral work by which he is best known—the piano suite *Pictures at an Exhibition* in the orchestration by Ravel, which sounds better than the original—contains none. And Rimsky-Korsakov, most prolific of the group, worked for the most part with original material in folk style, much of it influenced by the jingle and languor of the music of Asian lands in or bordering Russia, where tempers are warmer and dancing girls more sinuous.

The point is not whether these pioneers in the establishment of a possible music for their country did or did not borrow from folk sources, but what they accomplished overall. There was no actual physical place where the Five met and laid down rules for a cultural revolution; they were five friends, working around St. Petersburg at the same time, joined by a common cause, and creating their own music, but helping each other out. Rimsky-Korsakov, the master among the group in matters of brilliant (if occasionally rather blatant) orchestration, was called upon several times to complete scores left unfinished, or unworkable, by Borodin and Mussorgsky. The world still argues whether Rimsky's emendations to Borodin's *Prince Igor* and Mussorgsky's *Boris Godunov* did these works harm or good.

Tchaikovsky, Russia's other great composer of the time, did not join the group, and enjoyed a certain amount of their scorn for his major symphonic works, which were still fed from the pipeline running from Western ideals. Yet, in the long run, Tchaikovsky's personal success buttressed the work of the militant musical nationalists; he was a better composer than all five together, which is neither here nor there. What is important is that all six created a Russian music that continues to our time along lines that can easily be traced. Igor Stravinsky studied with Rimsky-Korsakov, but demonstrated in much of his music a frank adoration for Tchaikovsky. Thus, in the genius of our own day, the hostile factions are reconciled.

SELECTED RECORDINGS

Balakirev
Symphony No. 1 in C
  –Sir Thomas Beecham and the Royal Philharmonic
  Orchestra (Seraphim/HMV)

Borodin
**Symphony No. 2 in B Minor; Prince Igor Overture
and Dances**
  –Andrew Davis and the Toronto Symphony
  (Columbia)

Mussorgsky
Orchestral Music (complete)
  –Eugene Svetlanov and the USSR Symphony
  (Melodiya/HMV)
Pictures at an Exhibition (arr. Ravel)
  –Zubin Mehta and the Los Angeles Philharmonic
  Orchestra (London/Decca)

Rimsky-Korsakov
Antar (Symphony No. 2)
  –Maurice Abravanel and the Utah Symphony
  (Vanguard)
Sheherazade
  –Leonard Bernstein and the New York
  Philharmonic (Columbia)
  –Leopold Stokowski and the London Symphony
  (London/Decca)

This is all music fraught with temptations to overdramatize; the best performances, without exception, are those in which the rhythm is kept firm, and the orchestra so well controlled that the heavy coloration is not blurred. Generally speaking, Russian orchestras are not adequate in this music for Western ears; the brass, in particular, have a way of spreading the vibrato until the music sounds frantic and watery at the same time. Yet, a strong conductor can control these problems, and Svetlanov does in his disk of Mussorgsky (including the famous *Night on Bald Mountain*, which is actually an interlude from the opera *Fair at Sorotchinsk*.)

Mehta and Bernstein have a ball with this repertoire, for reasons explained under Liszt a few pages back. So does Sir Thomas Beecham in the Balakirev symphony, a work he resuscitated from neglect and promoted practically single-handedly. But the greatest romp among the above listings is that enjoyed by the venerable Stokowski in *Sheherazade*, an outrageously free performance of music that can take it. And when you've enjoyed this revel, try the less-familiar *Antar*, another score full of Rimsky's brilliant oriental palette, but shorter and, dare one suggest, just a little tidier than the *Sheherazade*.

Peter Ilyitch Tchaikovsky

b Orianenburg, Russia, May 7, 1840; *d* Moscow, November 7, 1893. Principal output includes: six symphonies; three piano concertos; violin concerto and other concerted works; symphonic poems (*Romeo and Juliet, Francesca da Rimini, 1812, Manfred*; ballets (*Swan Lake, The Sleeping Beauty, The Nutcracker*); operas (*Eugene Onegin, Pique Dame*); chamber music; piano works; songs; and choruses.

As with many 19th-century Romantics, the details of Tchaikovsky's life and character are as tumultuous as the music, and often inseparable from it. Yet these details—his hypersensitivity, his struggle with his homosexuality that drove him into a brief, disastrous marriage, the mysterious relationship with an adoring patroness whom he never met, the suicide attempts—all this too easily obscures the essential Tchaikovsky, the serious man of music, devoted to his craft and possessed of one of the greatest melodic gifts of all time.

When Tchaikovsky began to compose, native Russian art in all fields was still in its infancy, but, thanks to Pushkin's novels and the operas of Mikhail Glinka, had begun to be attended to in the West. Tchaikovsky's own contemporaries, the so-called Russian

89

"Five," were obsessed with establishing a "pure" national musical expression, free from the shadow of Western European techniques. Tchaikovsky stood somewhat apart. He avidly absorbed European ideals; his large-scale symphonies are planned along Western lines. Yet their vitality is the result of Tchaikovsky's peerless gift for creating a personal melodic style of irresistible sweep, colored but not dominated by Russian folksong and dance, and also colored by an astonishing command of orchestral nuance.

In all his music Tchaikovsky achieved an amalgam of formalism and personality. The casual listener might be tempted to downgrade surface traits in his music: the heart-on-sleeve soaring melodies in his great last symphony (which he himself dubbed the *Pathétique*), or the pure virtuosic display in the first Piano Concerto; these qualities have also proved fatally tempting to some performers looking for the easy success. But repeated hearings will easily reveal the depths and range of expression in Tchaikovsky's music. And in one genre in which his inspiration has never been in dispute, his ballet scores, a side of Tchaikovsky is revealed that could easily be overlooked: his command of the most understated grace and elegance, the unerring sense of proportion that betrays his lifelong reverence for the music of Mozart.

Composers since Tchaikovsky's time, Igor Stravinsky, in particular, have freely acknowledged their debt to their musical ancestor. One or two casual samplings of Tchaikovsky—the fierce syncopations at the climax of *Romeo and Juliet*, or the pounding rhythms in the finale of the neglected tone poem *Manfred*—suffice to reveal broad musical horizons beyond his own music awareness.

SELECTED RECORDINGS

Symphony No. 2 in C minor
   –Leonard Bernstein and the New York
   Philharmonic (Angel)

Symphony No. 6 in B minor *(Pathétique)*
   –Carlo Maria Giulini and the Philharmonica
   Orchestra (Seraphim/HMV)
   –Wilhelm Furtwängler and the Berlin Philharmonic
   (Seraphim)

Manfred
  –Lorin Maazel and the Vienna Philharmonic
  (London/Decca)
Romeo and Juliet (fantasy overture)
  –Claudio Abbado and the Boston Symphony
  (Deutsche Grammophon)
Swan Lake (complete or excerpts)
  –Gennadi Rozhdestvensky and the Moscow
  Philharmonic (Angel/HMV)

Piano Concerto No. 1 in B-flat minor
  –Vladimir Ashkenazy, pianist, with Lorin Maazel
  and the London Symphony (London/Decca)

Tchaikovsky's music is as treacherous to perform as any composer's in history. Its great moments fairly scream to be milked dry; yet the essence of Tchaikovsky—no less than that of Beethoven—is in the surging, irresistibly ongoing line, and this is the element that demands the greatest skill from any conductor or soloist. But then there can be the opposite pitfall, the temptation to make the music move so precipitously as to lose its radiance. Two of the most eloquent Tchaikovsky performances ever recorded—both, incidentally, of his orchestral masterpiece, Symphony No. 6—are by conductors not automatically associated with the Russian repertoire: Giulini and (in a performance recorded in 1938 but still available on a reissue) Furtwängler. In both performances there seems to be the initial premise that this is music of extraordinary depth and grandeur.

The early Symphony No. 2 (subtitled *The Little Russian*) is a dazzling and often witty score that seems to prefigure both the symphonic and balletic mature composer; it deserves to be better known. A complete *Swan Lake* may seem, for merely a listening experience, like too much of a good thing, yet any one act heard complete is remarkably well constructed. The particular *Manfred* and *Romeo* recordings are chosen, from among many competitors, as examples of especially clear-eyed and vivid readings, while Ashkenazy's eminently sensible reading of the well-known Piano Concerto keeps the music moving even when Tchaikovsky, as he does once in a while here, loses his way.

Anton Bruckner

b Ansfelden, Upper Austria, September 4, 1824; *d* Vienna, October 11, 1896. Principal output includes: nine symphonies (plus one bearing the number zero, predating these by two years); three masses and a Te Deum, plus considerable quantities of choral and organ music intended for church use; a string quintet; and miscellaneous small pieces of little importance.

At the height of his fame, Bruckner would stop in the middle of teaching a class in Vienna to kneel for the Angelus. Religion and music were the focal points of his existence, and the two for him were inseparable. His last symphony bears the dedication "to the beloved God," and the first eight might have borne the same inscription. Bruckner only really wrote "one" symphony, which he worked over in nine incarnations. The basic Bruckner symphony begins with an ominous murmur, usually in the tremolando strings (obviously an effect appropriated from the opening of Beethoven's Ninth). It portends vast horizons, the way ahead filled with massive and self-contained blocks of slow-treading harmonic themes, built up as they might be on an organ. These repeat in stepwise progression, building toward a brassy climax followed by a pause, almost as if the composer shared his audience's curiosity as to what might happen next.

Bruckner's themes themselves often seem to have come out of a provincial hymnal. For lightness he will introduce something like a flat-footed peasant dance. Yet there are also the slow movements, and here his symphonies reach their artistic climax, of a nobility and grandeur worthy of Beethoven. The finales are often anticlimactic, however, sometimes returning material from the first movement transformed, often trivialized. At the end, however, there is invariably a huge peroration, a brass-plated stairway to heaven stretching beyond sight.

Yet, there are distinctions among the various symphonies. The Third, which Bruckner dedicated to Wagner (it was only grudgingly accepted), has some interesting chromatic turns worthy of its recipient. The fourth, sometimes known as the *Romantic*, has a beautiful, serene opening; Bruckner wrote of it "the mood of a medieval city: morning light—morning trumpet calls—the city gates open — the knights ride out into the countryside—the magic of the forest surrounds them. . . ." Well and good, but the end betrays the mood.

The Eighth is much graver stuff. The key is C minor—Beethoven's key for demons. The slow movement is on a level of solemn mastery that Beethoven might have admired; you have to go to the adagio of Beethoven's own *Hammerklavier* sonata to find its equal. The Ninth presents a dilemma. Bruckner died before even sketching a final movement, although he suggested that performances might end with his choral work *Te Deum*. Current practice favors ending with the slow movement, which, as in the *Unfinished* of Franz Schubert, is so transfiguring that—post facto reasoning or not—no more music is needed.

Among past masters, Bruckner especially revered the ghost of Beethoven, though his idolatry did not bring him to the kind of grief encountered by Johannes Brahms. Bruckner never achieved the closely argued, dramatic rhetoric of either of these composers. His enthusiasts will point out the obvious (which he never cared to) that, as one writer puts it, Bruckner's aesthetic is that of "contemplative magnificence beyond the battle." His detractors are more likely to echo the words of Eduard Hanslick, who, in reviewing the Seventh Symphony, complained of "interminable stretches of darkness, leaden boredom and feverish over-excitement." It is doubtful that Bruckner will ever gain universal acceptance. The scale of his symphonies, like Mahler's, requires a patience not everyone is willing to afford. Depending where you stand, contemplative magnificence can sound rather self-indulgent.

SELECTED RECORDINGS

Symphony No. 3 in D minor
  –George Szell and the Cleveland Orchestra
  (Columbia)
Symphony No. 4 in E-flat major (*Romantic*)
  –Bruno Walter and the Columbia Symphony
  (Odyssey/CBS)
Symphony No. 7 in E major
  –Bernard Haitink and the Amsterdam
  Concertgebouw Orchestra (Philips)
Symphony No. 8 in C minor
  –Wilhelm Furtwängler and the Vienna
  Philharmonia Orchestra (EMI)
Symphony No. 9 in D minor
  –Carlo Maria Giulini and the Chicago Symphony
  Orchestra (Angel)

Shortest of the symphonies, the Third is recommended for people with reservations about Bruckner, and Szell works architectural wonders even in the sections where construction is creaky. The Fourth provides just the kind of radiant, dreamy music that Bruno Walter interprets better than anyone else. The Seventh is probably the most often played of the nine; the adagio is so clearly modeled after the slow movement of Beethoven's Ninth as to be amusing; it works best in the dryish Haitink treatment.

Furtwängler's magisterial performance of the Eighth is far outstripped in sound by any number of fine modern recordings, but the visionary intensity of his performance makes any other reading sound mild-mannered. Then there is the Giulini Ninth—extremely slow as is often this conductor's wont, but with that fiery, singing line that gives a Giulini performance momentum at any speed.

Gustav Mahler

b Kalischt, Bohemia, July 7, 1860; *d* Vienna, May 18, 1911. Principal output includes: nine symphonies (plus a tenth left incomplete but capable of completion); three orchestral song cycles plus a great many individual songs with piano or

orchestral accompaniment; *Das Klagende Lied* **for chorus and orchestra; and early chamber music of little consequence.**

"My time will come," Mahler said; if he only knew how! In the past two decades no composer's stock has risen more sharply. Today, only the symphonies of Beethoven, Brahms, and Tchaikovsky rival those of Mahler's in frequency of performance. Moreover, even to those who are not particularly interested in classical music, Mahler's flamboyant, highly agitated scores, their nerves raw and exposed, seem to elicit tremendous emotional empathy.

The Mahler cult has grown parallel to the advent of the virtuoso modern orchestra and the superstar conductor. No music is better suited to showing off the full range of an orchestra's ability and the wide gamut of a conductor's temperament. Whereas the music of Mozart, for instance, demands that its interpreters purge themselves of impure instincts, Mahler practically begs for emotional excess. Analyzing and comparing the relative merits of the way that a Bernstein, a Solti, a Mehta, or a Haitink ride to victory or defeat on the heels of one of Mahler's huge four-, five-, or six-act dramas has become a major cultural pastime.

"I am thrice homeless. As a Bohemian born in Austria. As an Austrian among Germans. And as a Jew throughout the world." Mahler's music offers a panacea to anyone who has ever entertained feelings of persecution or alienation. His critics will say that he sublimates these emotions, encouraging the listener to an orgy of empathetic self-pity. His symphonies, they say, contain many beautiful things, but also long stretches in which the interest lapses completely followed by passages of self-indulgent breast-beating and gratuitous striving for effect.

None of these arguments, whatever their applicability to the symphonies, can be leveled against the orchestral song cycles. Like most Romantics, Mahler was essentially a miniaturist, far more effective when he was content to be intimate and lyrical rather than monumental. In his late masterpiece *Das Lied von der Erde* (The Song of the Earth), a huge song cycle based on old Chinese poems in German translations, Mahler manages to be both simultaneously. Here, and in the Ninth Symphony, he achieved a distillation of technique that transcends the limitations of many of his earlier large-scale works.

Yet, though the earlier symphonies have become most famous for their length, and for the amount of self-indulgent, self-pitying, and self-confessed autobiographical material that Mahler crammed into them, they also show his intimate and lyrical side. He calls for a huge orchestra in all his works (including, in the Sixth Symphony, a set of cowbells to represent his bucolic boyhood and, in the Second, Third, and Eighth symphonies, huge choral aggregations, plus soloists). To refute the accusation of gigantism even further, there is the exquisite Fourth Symphony (small scale: it runs less than an hour!), which trails off into a soprano's song, to the most delicate orchestration, about a child's picture of heaven.

The Mahler revival has allowed us to reevaluate his influence on 20th-century music. His delicate orchestral effects certainly prefigure the experiments with orchestral color in early works of all three Viennese atonalists, and even seem to foreshadow some of Debussy's late scores. His harmony, furthering to some extent Wagner's inherent challenge to tonality and the need for central keys, is clearly a link between the 19th and 20th centuries. As far as the emotional angst of his music goes, most 20th-century composers have turned away from this quality with increasing disdain. Perhaps it is no coincidence that the rise in Mahler's popularity directly parallels the rejection by much of the public of the dry and cerebral in new music.

SELECTED RECORDINGS

Symphony No. 1 in D major
  –Bruno Walter and the Columbia Symphony
  Orchestra (Odyssey/CBS)

Symphony No. 3 in D minor
–Maureen Forrester, contralto, with Bernard
Haitink and a chorus and the Amsterdam
Concertgebouw Orchestra (Philips)

Symphony No. 4 in G major
–Frederica von Stade, soprano, with Claudio
Abbado and the Vienna Philharmonic Orchestra
(Deutsche Grammophon)

Symphony No. 5 in C-sharp minor
–Bruno Walter and the New York Philharmonic
Orchestra (Columbia)

Symphony No. 9 in D major
–Carlo Maria Giulini and the Chicago Symphony
Orchestra (Deutsche Grammophon)

Das Lied von der Erde
–Janet Baker and James King, soloists, with
Bernard Haitink and the Amsterdam
Concertgebouw Orchestra (Philips)
–Kathleen Ferrier and Julius Patzak, soloists, with
Bruno Walter and the Vienna Philharmonic
Orchestra (London)

Bruno Walter was the foremost champion of Mahler's
music in Mahler's own time, and remained so until his
death in 1962. Shortly before his death, Walter made
many luminous recordings of Mahler's music, with an
orchestra not totally responsive perhaps, but at least
capable. The finest of the extant Walter performances,
however, is the 1952 monaural recording made in Vienna of *Das Lied von der Erde*, with the incredibly powerful voice of Kathleen Ferrier in the three sections for
contralto.

Of the other conductors listed, both Haitink and
Giulini have become exceptionally wise performers of
this music, better able than most of their colleagues to
control the music's volcanic passions. Merely as beautiful sound, the combination of Giulini and the Chicago Symphony is an experience not to be missed.

SUPPLEMENTARY COMPOSERS

Georges Bizet (1838–1875)
Symphony in C major
–Bernard Haitink and the Amsterdam
Concertgebouw Orchestra (Philips)

Emmanuel Chabrier (1841–1894)
Complete music for orchestra (including *Bourrée
Fantasque, Suite Pastorale, Marche Joyeuse*)
–Louis de Froment and the Radio Luxembourg
Orchestra (Turnabout)

César Franck (1822–1890)
Symphony in D minor
–Pierre Monteux and the Chicago Symphony
Orchestra (RCA)

Edvard Grieg (1843–1907)
Piano Concerto in A minor
–Gina Bachauer, pianist, with George Weldon and
the Royal Philharmonic Orchestra (Seraphim)

Moritz Moszkowski (1854–1925)
Piano Concerto in E major
–Michel Ponti, pianist, with the Philharmonia
Hungarica (Candide/Vox)

Camille Saint-Saëns (1835–1921)
Piano Concerto No. 4 in C minor
–Robert Casadesus, pianist, with Leonard Bernstein
and the New York Philharmonic (Columbia)

Every musical period produces its share of bad art
along with the great, but it's safe to say that bad, or at
least second-rate, music from the Romantic era is
probably more enjoyable than the routine output of
any other era. That is, of course, because the prime
aim of all Romantic composers was to communicate
directly into the heart and circulatory system of the
idealized listener, who, in turn, was fancied as a per-
sonage of maximum vulnerability. Thus, the poorer
works of the Romantic era are, at the very least, full of
attractive material—either not very well arranged by

their composers or mixed with so many other elements as to lose any sense of individuality.

The César Franck symphony (and the other symphonies it spawned—by Ernest Chausson, Vincent d'Indy, and Camille Saint-Saëns) is awful only because its agreeable, quasi-religious tunes are so heavily overlain with ill-planned obeisances to the Wagnerian aesthetic as to lose all individuality. The evergreen Piano Concerto of Grieg, like all his music, pleasantly strains to embrace a sense of Norwegian national expression, but falls apart eventually because of its worship of such central European models as the concerto of Robert Schumann. The Fourth Piano Concerto (the best of five) by the prolific Saint-Saëns is pretty, dreamy, and, at the end, bravely rhetorical; its main failing is its slavish attempts to translate the plan of the Liszt symphonic poem, transformation of themes and all, into a style whose themes appear silly in any but their original form.

Against all this struggling, the totally adorable little symphony of Bizet, a schoolboy work full of deep bows to classicism, stands out by virtue of its honesty and the vitality of its material, including, as its second movement, a melodic arch of unforgettable poignancy clearly delineated. Likewise, the manic vulgarity of Chabrier's music, much of it shamelessly stolen from Russian models, is managed with such wit that even such warhorses as the *España* rhapsody hold a deserved place in the affections.

Finally, the Piano Concerto by the otherwise almost-forgotten Moszkowski deals with the nature of Romantic virtuosity with such geniality, such a wealth of pure featherbrained oratory, that its effect can be almost narcotic. It has that quality—shared by the Bizet symphony—of worming its way into the affections against all common sense.

The Twentieth Century

By 1900, the symphony orchestra had become firmly established in the cultural life of Western society, from Moscow to San Francisco. Its place as the central adornment of a city's musical life was challenged only by the local opera company. The European musical capitals—London, Paris, Berlin, and Vienna—boasted four or five full-time orchestras each. In the United States, too, most major cities had symphony orchestras by 1900: Boston, New York, Philadelphia, Washington, Chicago, St. Louis, and San Francisco. New York's Philharmonic is generally reckoned as the oldest American orchestra; it was founded in 1842, although in that year its entire season consisted of four concerts. Compare that with the nearly 200 concerts that same orchestra presents today!

The orchestra in the 19th century, as we have already seen, grew not only in quantity but, more importantly, in size, in variety of musical physiognomy, and in virtuosity. The greatest composers in terms of pure orchestral resource, from Beethoven through Berlioz to Wagner and Mahler, constantly demanded of the orchestra more than it had previously given. By the end of the century, it was reasonable to wonder how much further the orchestra could develop before it—or the sounds it made—became too big to fit into existing concert halls.

The last symphonies of Gustav Mahler, whose career began in the 19th century but who, strictly speaking, created many of his most individualistic large-scale works in the first decade of the 20th, were created on the premise that there was nothing the hundred-odd musicians of a symphony orchestra could not express—the most personal pained outcry, the exultation of Judgment Day, the faintest murmur from the stillness of a rural landscape. Few composers after Mahler dared to extend very much further the paths suggested in his late symphonies. There seemed in some quarters, in fact, a conscious desire—brought on to some extent by the normal wave of self-consciousness that accompanied the dawn of a new century—to reexamine the state of music and to consider possible new beginnings.

Nowhere was this more true than in Germany and Austria, where the symphonic tradition had been the most firmly rooted. The Vienna-born Arnold Schoenberg had met Mahler in 1903, and the older composer was warmly supportive of Schoenberg's early works, which, truth to tell, were strongly under the Mahlerian spell. But Schoenberg, along with his Viennese disciples Alban Berg and Anton von Webern, soon moved far along new paths, and a major part of their pioneering zeal stemmed from a conscious disavowal of what had been accepted previously as basic musical truths. And it is interesting that all three composers, early in their careers, turned out sets of pieces for orchestra that seemed like conscious disavowals of Mahlerian gigantism: short, coloristic exercises that sought to explore the clear, small orchestral sonorities, the "primary colors," to draw an analogy from the visual arts.

Almost at the same time, the Russian émigré Igor Stravinsky, working in Paris with the great Diaghilev Ballet, was also exploring his own new paths. A pupil of Rimsky-Korsakov, and therefore an heir to the brilliant, Romantic orchestral language of 19th-century Russia, Stravinsky took explosive leave of his forbears in his extraordinary *Rite of Spring* of 1913, in which virtually every classic way of regarding the orchestra was overturned. Although Stravinsky himself almost never returned to the iconoclastic orchestral manner of this milestone masterpiece, many suggestions in *The Rite of Spring*—the way, for example, that the string section is dismissed from its usual function as bearer of melody and made to act like a kind of percussion—had a strong influence on other composers of this century, most notably the Hungarian Béla Bartók.

This is not to say, of course, that all musical traditions, everywhere in the world, were suddenly and purposely severed at the dawn of the 20th century. Musical history has always revolved around a running battle between the conservatives and the progressives, those who want to continue creation in familiar (and, for the most part, lucrative!) styles and those who must forge ahead. Beethoven and Schubert, as the progressives of their day, had to struggle for recognition against the dominance of the less adventurous, and more popular, contemporary composers; the great Wagner-Brahms tempest that shattered teapots in the 1870s was more of the same. And the rise of the "new" music—actually, of course, many kinds of new music—in our own century was opposed, by word or simply by example, from the organized and respectable conservative camp.

Thus, while Schoenberg and his school were incurring ire in Vienna and Berlin, while Stravinsky was laying siege to Parisian equanimity, while another group of young Parisians called, simply, the "Six" (Darius Milhaud, Francis Poulenc, Arthur Honegger, George Auric, Louis Durey, and Germaine Tailleferre) were also rocking the French establishment by introducing such "daring" elements as Brazilian dance rhythms and American jazz into their serious compositions, just as many distinguished composers were seeking a more amicable reconciliation with the artistic aims of the past.

To England, for example, the jolly baronet Sir Edward Elgar brought the German spirit of symphonic style, and as late as 1930 he continued to write resolutely old-fashioned symphonies, tone poems, and concert overtures full of a Brahmsian heartiness. His musical descendants, Ralph Vaughan Williams and William Walton (also both eventually knighted), added to the Elgarian rhetoric a touch of more national flavor, from their studies in traditional British folk and popular music. To the north, Jan Sibelius reflected the spirit of national expression in symphonic language that, generations before, had motivated the likes of Dvořák and the Russian "Five." In the Soviet Union, too, the large-scale symphonic output of two major composers, Sergei Prokofiev and Dmitri Shostakovich, can be regarded as continuations of the Russian symphonic tradition that had begun with Tchaikovsky and the "Five" late in the 19th century.

For such composers the symphony orchestra remained a prime medium, and composers like Vaughan Williams, Sibelius, and Shostakovich lived pretty much the heroes' lives that Brahms and Tchaikovsky had enjoyed before them. To such composers as the Viennese atonalists and, until late in their lives, Bartók and Stravinsky, however, the orchestra was less readily accessible. The split between conservative and progressive had spread in a sense to the symphonic audience. Unlike the situation in most major cities in, say, 1875, where the audience lived for the latest symphony or concerto by the reigning hero, the 20th-century symphonic audience began to live increasingly in the past and to develop a passion for the familiar. The growth of the phonograph record and the high-fidelity industry after the Second World War added to this obsession to take refuge in history. With few exceptions, the most progressive composers of the midcentury were writing less for large orchestra and more for small ensemble.

Nowhere was this more evident than in the United States, where orchestras were supported far more from private contributions, which meant, more often than not, contributions from older patrons whose tastes could be expected to be conservative. Although there were the beginnings of an American orchestral repertoire in the 19th century, little of it proved to be of any importance other than historic: the work of well-trained academic musicians who went off to one or another German conservatory and came back writing good German music. The first important truly American composer trained to some extent in European precepts was Charles Ives. By 1916, Ives had already turned out a major repertoire of orchestral works—virtually none of which saw the light of the concert hall until nearly forty years later. Then, practically at death's door, known and respected by serious musicians the country over but hardly at all by the public, Ives began to hear his music played for the first time.

By the time of the Second World War, the United States had produced a respectable number of composers. The 1930s saw the development of an American symphonic repertoire. Composers like Roy Harris, Aaron Copland, and Virgil Thomson wrote in a tradition clearly traceable to the ideals of the European nationalists of the previous century. Their music, brilliant and edgy and sometimes taking on the movement of American pop styles, including jazz, still had a stylistic core that was beholden to the past, and it made easy headway—as did that of a younger, even more eclectic imitator, Leonard Bernstein. But a more serious corps of composers, striving somewhat harder than their colleagues to move stylistic boundaries forward, and to place the United States in the international musical mainstream, found it more difficult to gain access to the major orchestras, and it is unlikely that the immensely complex music of Elliott Carter or of Roger Sessions will ever achieve widespread acclaim.

Again, many of these composers, like their European counterparts, merely abandoned hope of entering the symphonic mainstream and developed a repertoire of works for smaller ensembles. One interesting alternative presented itself in the 1950s, however, and has been assiduously explored ever since: the idea of creating an almost infinite variety of sound—far more varied, potentially, than even the output of a great orchestra—produced by electronic means and turned into artistic designs, that is, compositions, by the composer working directly onto tape. At first, a great many composers tinkered with the electronic gadgetry and came up with not much more than an amusing collection of sounds. More recently, however, a serious output of electronic music has attracted considerable attention; the works of Morton Subotnick (1933–) have the breadth of sound and the depth of organization that we associate with the notion of "symphonic." Electronic technology has also enabled many composers to manipulate the sound of "normal" instruments; a single violin can, for example, undergo metamorphosis in a maze of computer circuitry and emerge sounding like a 200-member string section.

Ultimately, of course, it is the quality of the composer's design, not merely the novelty of his medium, that will decide the fate of electronic music. It was always so; the stature of Beethoven's *Eroica* was not merely that the composer had written an abnormally long symphony, or that he used the orchestra in a novel way, but that he made the length and sound of the work an inevitable adjunct to a great and original musical vision. That will also be the determining factor for the music of our own time.

Claude Achille Debussy

b St. Germain-en-Laye, August 22, 1862; *d* Paris, March 25, 1918. Principal output includes: orchestral works (three *Nocturnes*, the last with wordless chorus of women's voices; *La Mer*, *Images, Prelude to the Afternoon of a Faun*, and the ballet *Jeux*); the opera *Pelléas et Mélisande;* incidental music to d'Annunzio's *Martyrdom of St. Sebastian*; choral works; chamber music and music for piano solo and duet; and a great quantity of songs.

Journalists, and writers of listener's guides, are in constant need of easy catchwords to classify what they write about, and for the better part of a century the easiest catchword applied to Debussy's music was "Impressionist," thus creating a bond with the major French painters of his time. It is true that one aspect of Debussy's musical language has some relationship with the blurred outlines, the capturing of the evanescent play of light in the paintings of Monet and Cézanne. It would be possible, for example, to hear the play of indistinct melodic shapes across the surface of the orchestra in "Clouds," the first of Debussy's *Noc-*

turnes for orchestra, and feel an artistic oneness between this music and, say, one of Monet's studies of the Rouen Cathedral.

Yet, Debussy's style partakes of a great deal more than this one influence, important though it be. It is safe to say that no composer at the turn of the century reached out so hungrily, and with so great a range of imagination, to all that could come into his music and make it different, individual, and a step ahead of what had gone before. Debussy had always been like that; he rebelled, early in life, against the stiff academicism of César Franck's classes at the Paris Conservatory.

The young Debussy mingled with poets, including the naughty Baudelaire, Rimbaud, and Verlaine; he knew the painters of the time; he also, like his colleagues in the other expressive arts, took in with wonderment the music from Indonesia, India, and the Far East that came to Paris in the great World's Fair of 1889. He visited Bayreuth, was both thrilled and disturbed by Wagner's implications, and worked consciously to purge his music of Wagnerisms.

The synthesis that Debussy evolved as his own musical style partook, then, of the Impressionistic blurring that he saw in the paintings and heard in the poetry of the day, of the intricate, hypnotic patterns of Oriental music that could wind its langorous way for hours totally free of the harmonic system that the West regarded as crucial, and the supple rhythms and cadences of the French language, which he studied assiduously. Such a work as the *Prelude to the Afternoon of a Faun*, Debussy's first orchestral work, and the three sea pictures *La Mer*, his most popular, are most remarkable in the way they manage a complete freedom while maintaining a structure that creates on their own terms the rise and fall of traditional Western music. He worked with an exquisite ear for nuance and rivaled a musical rebel of a previous generation—Hector Berlioz—in the outpouring of sheer inventiveness to obtain an exact sound or effect.

Debussy never abandoned traditional tonality, although he had a marvelous command over devices to make it seem as if the music had, at least for a time, floated free of its harmonic moorings. Yet, it always returned. His range of color—even in his piano music,

and certainly in his orchestral works—was phenomenal, but he never made sheer color an end in itself, as
some of his Viennese colleagues were doing at the
time. His influence, as an innovator and as an artistic
eclectic in the best sense, was profound. No French
composer since his time—not even the avant-garde
Boulez or the most fervid creators of far-out French
jazz—fails to acknowledge that almost everything that
is being done today was done by Debussy, first.

SELECTED RECORDINGS

"Complete" Music for Orchestra
 —Pierre Boulez and the New Philharmonia and
 Cleveland Orchestras (three records; also available
 separately) (Columbia)
La Mer; Nocturnes
 —Carlo Maria Giulini and the Philharmonia
 Orchestra (Angel/HMV)
 —Charles Münch and the French National
 Orchestra (Turnabout)

The "complete" describing the Boulez set is actually
merely approximate, as the album doesn't include
such early works as the Fantaisie for Piano and Orchestra or the set of fragments from *The Martyrdom of
St. Sebastian* that others have recorded. But Boulez on
Debussy is like a genius of the present touching the
hand that guided him, and to hear the strength and
clarity of his presentation is to understand both Debussy and the vibrations that have passed from his
music to the innovators of the present (Boulez, of
course, included).

Yet there are those who prefer the traditional,
blurred, Romantic Debussy, and the late Charles
Münch played this music with sublime nobility and
elegance. And—as he does in the music of such other
"alien" cultures as the Czech and the Russian—Giulini
finds ways of unlocking secrets in Debussy, and his
performances are remarkable for their enormous ten-
sile strength, the inexorable building from whisper to
exultant shout (most of all in his incredible traversal
of *La Mer*).

Maurice Ravel

b Ciboure, Basses-Pyrénées, March 7, 1875; *d* Paris, December 28, 1937. Principal output includes: orchestral music (the ballets *Daphnis and Chloë, Mother Goose,* and *La Valse; Rhapsodie espagnol, Le Tombeau de Couperin, Boléro,* plus two piano concertos and *Tzigane* for violin and orchestra); the song cycle *Schéhérezade* for voice and orchestra; two one-act operas; chamber music, including cycles for voice and instruments; much piano music solo or duet; and songs.

Ravel matured in a music atmosphere dominated by Claude Debussy, thirteen years his senior; because the two were linked by proximity and respect, lazy writers often link their names. This is false; given the reverence Ravel felt toward the older composer, it is remarkable how quickly the younger man found his own voice. From the beginning, the concern in Ravel is for precision and clarity of form, as Debussy favors shadows. Ravel's music exists in daylight; its meaning is always clear, spelled out in unmistakable patterns by a meticulous craftsman. It is probably no accident that both his short operas are about clocks.

Ravel holds a special place in the annals of orchestral composers. His affinity for instruments, his ability to invent new, exquisite combinations of sounds, is second to none in musical history. The range of his subject matter is remarkably far-reaching, considering the relative paucity of his output. He worked happily in a Spanish vein, had a gift for satire and fantasy, and was fascinated with the waltz, classicism and antique modes of expression, and American jazz.

His orchestral masterpiece is undoubtedly the ballet *Daphnis and Chloë,* created in 1912 and soon to be overshadowed by Stravinsky's *Rite of Spring.* Yet *Daphnis* was also a revolutionary work, and for reasons other than its controversial use of a wordless choir (offstage) as an element of the orchestration. The nearly hour-length score embraces the most exquisite, quiet effects, as in the opening passage where the music seems to assemble itself over vast space, to the magical depiction of daybreak with its slowly coalescing rivulets of sound, to the neo-classic pantomime wherein Daphnis mimes the story of Pan to the sound of his flute, to the wild exaltation of the final "General Dance" with the same metrical flexibility that Stravinsky was to employ to no greater sensation a year later.

The most popular work is, of course, the notorious *Boléro* (conceived as a solo dance for the great Ida Rubinstein). Yet this work is itself a tour de force, a gigantic, meticulously controlled crescendo of an obsession, created by the gradual accumulation of orchestration and, therefore, of volume. Although it is seldom used that way, *Boléro* should be the supreme test of a conductor's self-control.

Late in life Ravel toured the United States as composer and pianist. American jazz had always interested him, as it had most of his French confrères; in 1923 he had written a blues movement into a violin sonata. The 1931 Piano Concerto was—along with Darius Milhaud's ballet *The Creation of the World*—the most successful integration of jazz rhythms and breaks into concert music, with the classic purity of the slow movement beautifully separating the two riotous outer sections. It, too, is something of a masterpiece.

SELECTED RECORDINGS

Daphnis and Chloë, complete ballet
–Pierre Boulez and the New York Philharmonic (Columbia/CBS)
–Jean Martinon and the Orchestre de Paris (Angel) (both with chorus)
Mother Goose (ballet); **Boléro**; **La Valse**
–Pierre Monteux and the London Symphony Orchestra (Philips)
Piano Concerto; **Concerto for Piano Left Hand**
–Aldo Ciccolini, pianist, with Jean Martinon and the Orchestre de Paris (Angel)
Alborada del Gracioso; Daphnis and Chloë Suite No. 2; Rhapsodie espagnole; Pavane for a Dead Infanta
–Carlo Maria Giulini and the Philharmonia Orchestra (EMI/HMV)

As with Debussy, there are two ways of playing Ravel's music successfully; bringing out with clinical accuracy the incredible details of his orchestration, or going for the lustrous sound at all costs. Both can be extremely exciting, as a comparison of the meticulous Boulez *Daphnis* performance to the ecstatic Martinon will indicate. The late Martinon was a splendid, sensible conductor of French music, and recorded the complete Ravel *oeuvre* just before his death. Ciccolini is an adept collaborator in the two brilliant concertos—the second a glistening, sinister work composed for the one-armed pianist Paul Wittgenstein.

As with other instances cited frequently throughout this book, performances by the late Pierre Monteux and by Carlo Maria Giulini tend to serve as the final refuge of sane, noble, unhurried eloquence, and such is the case here. It is remarkable how Monteux can take such a work as the much-played *Boléro* and make it sound as if he were conducting it for the first time and finds each page a new delightful surprise. The same goes for Giulini on his nobly played "greatest hits" collection.

Jan Sibelius

b Tavastehus, Finland, December 8, 1865; *d* Järvenpää, Finland, September 20, 1957. Principal output includes: orchestral music (seven symphonies, a violin concerto, sets of incidental music for plays, and a quantity of symphonic poems, many on subjects from Finnish legend); chamber music (including two string quartets); works for piano solo; the opera *The Maid in the Tower*; some choral music; and many songs.

Few composers in history have been accorded the honor in their native land that Jan Sibelius enjoyed in Finland during his lifetime. Part of this can be explained by Sibelius being the first composer in Finland's history to achieve international status, but it is more than that. Like Dvořák, in what is now Czechoslovakia, and like Verdi, and his operas in Italy, Sibelius lived during a time when the repressions of occupying forces—in his case, Russia's czarist regime—stirred patriotic feelings in the population. Sibelius drew upon his own fervent love of country to create descriptive works—the tone poem *Finlandia*, and the many works based on the traditional poetic cycle *Kalevala*—that embodied some sense, both vague and extremely tangible, of Finnish nationality. His seven symphonies, also, while admittedly not inspired by Finnish subjects, can easily be related to the look of the country—its wastelands, its vastness, the chill of its sunlight.

In the first few decades of this century, the music of Sibelius achieved a popularity in the United States that even surprised the composer himself. His music was hotly debated; a pro-Sibelius critic, the late Olin Downes of the *New York Times*, actually invoked the name of Beethoven, while his rival, Virgil Thomson of the *Herald-Tribune*, poured endless venom on the music.

Of all the symphonic works (the notoriously popular and populist *Finlandia* aside), the Second Symphony has always remained popular; its melodic outpourings, nameless griefs (in the slow movement), and brassy climax have seen to that. Now, however, there is a revival of all the symphonies. It has long been obvious that Sibelius is not the vital modern force his enthusiasts once claimed; he would gain, in fact, if some way were found to grant him honorary membership in the 19th century.

His music is, admittedly, riddled with mannerisms: the use, *ad tedium*, of short repeated fragments, the murky scoring in the low orchestral registers, the grandiose blasts from trumpets and trombones coming out of nowhere. Yet, there is a strong individualistic strain in his music. The major scores—the Fourth and Seventh symphonies and the tone poem *Pohjola's Daughter*—are elusive at first, due to the often elliptical, aphoristic treatment of wispy bits of melody. As the music moves on, these wisps come together and form grand melodies only at the end. (The slow movement of the Fourth Symphony is a marvelous example of this.)

And also, when their present excessive popularity dies down, there will be much beauty in the smaller works, the tone poems, even the blatant patriotic pageants. Such works, most of all the elegiac *Kalevala* fragment *The Swan of Tuonela*, will justifiably hold their place with the passage of time.

SELECTED RECORDINGS

Symphony No. 2 in D, Opus 36
   –Serge Koussevitzky and the Boston Symphony (RCA)
Symphony No. 4 in A minor, Opus 63
   –Colin Davis and the Boston Symphony (Philips)
Violin Concerto in D minor, Opus 47
   –Jascha Heifetz, with Walter Hendl and the Chicago Symphony (RCA)
Short Works (including *Finlandia*, *The Swan of Tuonela*)
   –Eugene Ormandy and the Philadelphia Orchestra (RCA)

Koussevitzky was one of Sibelius' first American champions, and his recording of the Second Symphony, though dating from the 1940s, has lost none of its stirring power, its sense of pleading a cause. Colin Davis is one of several conductors who have recently led a Sibelius rediscovery; his complete set of the symphonies (with the Boston Symphony) has earned justifiably extravagant praise. The Violin Concerto is an old-fashioned work, even for Sibelius; its slow movement seems to be one long breath of Tchaikovskian melody, and for this kind of music there can never be another Heifetz. Ormandy, another early Sibelius champion, is still a peerless interpreter of these rich, romantic scores.

Sergei Vassilievitch Rachmaninoff

b Novgorod, April 1, 1873; *d* Beverly Hills, March 28, 1943. Principal output includes: orchestral music (three symphonies, four piano concertos and the *Paganini Rhapsody*, tone poems, including *Isle of the Dead*, and *Three Symphonic Dances*); three operas; considerable choral music, including settings of Russian Orthodox chant; innumerable

**piano works, also two *Suites for Two Pianos*;
songs; chamber works; and transcriptions for piano
of anything and everything.**

A century that began with
the revolutions fomented by
Stravinsky, Schoenberg, and
Bartók also had room for Sergei Rachmaninoff, who studied with Tchaikovsky, carried
on from his master's style
(but without anything like
Tchaikovsky's versatility and
depth of expression), and
throughout his life wrote a great deal of highly proficient music that was set in styles considered hopeless-
ly conservative but that gave pleasure to a great many
people for perfectly respectable reasons.

Rachmaninoff's success with almost everything he
composed—once he overcame a large number of creative blocks through psychoanalysis—stands as important proof that the quality of a composer's work is
not automatically determined by his position along
the conservative-progressive spectrum. His music is
no less exalted, on its own terms, than any acknowledged masterpiece in the books; it's just that Rachmaninoff's only way of expressing exaltation was
through a soaring, sentimental melody. In his late
years he settled close to Hollywood. But as early as
1901, when Hollywood was empty farmland and *The
Great Train Robbery* was three years in the future, Rachmaninoff composed melodies in his Second Piano
Concerto that were to sustain the movie industry from
one banal epic to the next.

Rachmaninoff had a greater mastery than merely a
proficiency at thinking up tunes. The piano concertos—the Third better than the Second, perhaps—do
have a considerable sweep, and so for all its "mud and
sugar" (another critic's words) does the Second Symphony. And Rachmaninoff's last work for piano and
orchestra, the extraordinarily clever (and blessedly
concise) *Rhapsody on a Theme by Paganini* is a complex es-
say in the variation form that Brahms would have
gladly acknowledged.

SELECTED RECORDINGS

Piano Concerto No. 2 in C minor; Piano Concerto No. 3 in D minor
—Vladimir Ashkenazy, soloist, with Andre Previn and the London Symphony Orchestra (two separate records) (London/Decca)
—Sergei Rachmaninoff, soloist, with Leopold Stokowski and Eugene Ormandy and the Philadelphia Orchestra (RCA)

Piano Concerto No. 3 in D minor
—Vladimir Horowitz, soloist, with Eugene Ormandy and the New York Philharmonic Orchestra (RCA)

Symphony No. 2 in E minor
—Eugene Ormandy and the Philadelphia Orchestra (RCA)

Ashkenazy's warm, idiomatic accounts of the two best-known piano concertos show that this Russian-born pianist has this music in his blood. Yet, the spell of Rachmaninoff's own (ancient, of course) recordings with his "favorite" orchestra (and, presumably, his two "favorite" conductors) is strong, though the performances are strangely erratic and mannered. The essence of the Third Concerto is sheer bloodcurdling virtuosity. Vladimir Horowitz made his American career by trundling this work around, and still does; he plays the daylights out of it. Ormandy's performance was formed ages ago, under the composer's watchful eye, and hasn't changed a sixteenth-note since.

Richard Strauss

b Munich, June 11, 1864; *d* Garmisch-Partenkirchen, September 8, 1949. Principal output includes: orchestral music (two youthful symphonies; concertos for violin, oboe, French horn, and the *Burleske* for piano and orchestra; a large number of symphonic poems on diverse subjects; two ballets; a set of incidental pieces to Molière's *Le Bourgeois Gentilhomme* for small orchestra, based on music by Lully; two sets for small orchestra of transcriptions from keyboard pieces by Couperin; a suite of orchestral pieces

**derived from the opera *Der Rosenkavalier*;
countless marches, waltzes, fanfares for public
occasions); fifteen operas; choral music and part
songs; chamber and piano music, most of it
youthful; a large number of songs with piano or
orchestral accompaniment.**

His father was a Munich horn
player who, the story goes,
had shown Wagner how to
write the horn call for Siegfried in *The Ring*; yet the elder
Strauss claimed his own son's
music was beyond him. It was
beyond many people at the
beginning, when the young
Strauss, producing a series of
glistening orchestral sym-
phonic poems with stunning facility, found himself
proclaimed on all sides as the genius who would pick
up Wagner's fallen torch.

Through that series of symphonic poems, all of
them written between 1888 and 1902, and into the
dazzling excitement of the early operas *Elektra* and *Salo-
me*, it looked very much as if Strauss was marshaling
his musical forces to advance the musical horizons beyond even Wagnerian lines. But then, something went
sour, or, more to the point, sweet. *Der Rosenkavalier*,
with its evocations of Mozart's Vienna garishly
touched up with sentimental waltzes, had (and main-
tains) a certain infectious charm, but then came decline. The still-young master began to rewrite himself,
seldom to his betterment. He turned out opera after
opera, and many still hold the affection of European
audiences; there is little chance, however, that the rest
of the world has sold Strauss short. At the end, after
the collapse of his Germany (in whose activities he
participated, if not wholeheartedly), there was a twilight glow: an oboe concerto (with small orchestra) of
some charm and some radiantly beautiful songs.

But the orchestral Strauss ceased to exist, at least as
a potent force, after 1902. Before then, to be sure, he
had created some leaping, striding near-masterpieces:
the symphonic poem *Till Eulenspiegel's Merry Pranks*,
with its jouncing themes and its evocation of rural

folkways; the distillation of Don Juan's search for the Eternal Feminine, in music that moves ever upward without ever finding melodic fulfillment; the pure egocentricity of *A Hero's Life*, in which Strauss himself is the hero, and his critics a bunch of cacklers; the splendid fantasy of *Don Quixote*, the woeful knight·impersonated by a solo cello coming up against realistic musical depictions of braying sheep, the arms of a windmill, a buxom country wench. Strauss is supposed once to have held up a fork, when asked what the highest aim of music should be, and announced that his highest aim was to compose fork music that could never be mistaken for a spoon.

Stylistically, his music is actually a throwback to well before the innovations of Wagner. His harmony is simple; it is the overlay of extraneous effects that gives it the impression of dissonance. Some of it is, to be sure, extraordinarily beautiful; when, at the end of *Don Quixote*, the tired old man retires from his adventures and quietly accepts death, the gallivanting theme for solo cello that has been his nametag is simplified down to a haunting, radiant song. There was some good in a man who could write such music, and there are moments like that in all of Strauss, here and there. And there is that phenomenal orchestral bedazzlement—all that Strauss must be granted.

SELECTED RECORDINGS

Don Juan; Till Eulenspiegel; Also Sprach Zarathustra
  –Sir Georg Solti and the Chicago Symphony Orchestra (London/Decca)

Don Quixote
  –Mstislav Rostropovitch, cello, with Herbert von Karajan and the London Philharmonic Orchestra (Angel/HMV)

Ein Heldenleben
  –Sir Thomas Beecham and the Royal Philharmonic Orchestra (Angel/EMI)
  –Willem Mengelberg and the New York Philharmonic-Symphony Orchestra (RCA)

Horn Concertos Nos. 1 and 2
  –Barry Tuckwell, horn, with Istvan Kertesz and the
  London Symphony Orchestra (London/Decca)

Adequate performances of this music demand, at best,
a somewhat impatient temperament that will not be
tempted to dawdle as the demonic Strauss brandishes
bouquets of langour. There is a fine drive, a hectic
pacing, in the Solti and Karajan approaches, often out
of place in some music but here exactly right. If you
crave a recording of *Also sprach Zarathustra* because of
the appearance of its first two minutes in *2001*, be
warned that that music doesn't return, and that there
are some thirty more minutes in the piece of somewhat lesser distinction.

  The great Beecham had a way with *Ein Heldenleben*;
he could almost make the music presentable in mixed
company, without minimizing its color, and his recording, from 1947, is still worth hearing. The ancient
Mengelberg performance, from 1927, is dim-sounding
but potent, for it was to Mengelberg that Strauss dedicated the score.

  The First Horn Concerto is a work of Strauss's
youth: a lovely one-movement workout for the soloist
to music of great vitality. Play it without identifying
it; your friends are likely to guess anyone from around
1830, but never Strauss. That may not be a detraction.

THE
VIENNESE ATONALISTS

Arnold Schoenberg
b Vienna, September 13, 1874;
d Los Angeles, July 13, 1951

Anton Webern
b Vienna, December 3, 1883;
d Mittersill, Austria, September 15, 1945

Alban Berg
b Vienna, February 9, 1885;
d Vienna, December 24, 1935

Principal output includes: orchestral works (sets of short pieces by all three composers; violin concertos by Schoenberg and Berg; also by Schoenberg: the symphonic poem *Pelleas and Melisande*, orchestrations of his sextet *Transfigured Night*, and the first Chamber Symphony); operas by Schoenberg: three short musical dramas and the full-length opera *Moses and Aaron* (unfinished); by Berg: the operas *Wozzeck* and *Lulu* (unfinished); by all three: a quantity of chamber music for various combinations; piano pieces; songs; and choral works.

Arnold Schoenberg

The young Arnold Schoenberg showed talent: a good violinist and an interesting composer in the style of Brahms and perhaps a little beyond. Parents and friends encouraged him; he turned out a decent repertoire of songs and piano pieces, starting at about age 20. At the age of 26, in 1900, he succumbed to the musical gigantism in the air—Mahler, Strauss, and figures now unknown—and began a gigantic cantata based on Danish poetry, called *Gurre-Lieder* and retelling a bloody medieval legend that might have turned Franz Liszt gray. A year later, the work was finished; in it were the signs of Romanticism at its ripest, and also an implied acceptance of the fact that the style could go no farther.

In 1903, Schoenberg met the younger composer Alban Berg, who had heard Schoenberg's music and came begging for lessons. By 1906, Schoenberg was teaching composition at the University of Vienna, where his students included, in addition to Berg, another intense young Viennese, Anton von Webern. (He later dropped the "von.") These young men were drawn together, and to their teacher, by the knowledge that it was absolutely necessary to give birth to a new music.

The relationship among the three soon passed from teacher-pupil to co-revolutionist. All three composers knew that the "old order" had come to an end with Wagner, just as Siegfried had shattered the spear of Wotan at the midpoint of *The Ring*. They applied themselves to a systematic examination of what elements from the old language could be kept and what had lost their importance. The decision was not so much a resolution to act, to destroy, as it was a recognition of what had already happened.

Tristan und Isolde had drawn the curtain on the new music; that much was clear. Five hours of music with virtually no coming-to-rest in a given key, no harmonic system that clearly defined the progression from chord to chord—that was enough in itself to suggest that the sanctity of a harmonic system to which lip service had been paid for two centuries had come to the end of its usefulness. In 1909, Schoenberg composed his *Five Pieces for Orchestra* in which the classic harmonic sense was all but inaudible; one of the pieces, in fact, consisted of a single chord oozing, growing, diminishing, through the orchestral texture. Webern wrote his *Six Pieces for Orchestra* two years later; like Schoenberg's, they drew their form from orchestral color, not from melody or harmony or repetition of phrase. Webern's pieces, moreover, were infinitesimally small; tiny dabs of color against a background of silence. The progression from one dab of color to another, he said, was a kind of melody ("tone-color melody") in itself. Berg's *Three Orchestral Pieces* followed in 1913; warmer and more robust in tone, but equally beholden to Schoenberg's guiding premise that the harmonic basis was no longer the way to make music work.

Anton Webern

The small, strange noises made by these men—supported by some central European intellectuals, hooted down by others—were in fact akin to movements in other arts. The Russian émigré Wassily Kandinsky spoke, in Munich in 1910, about the self-sufficiency of art, about the spirituality of red or yellow or of unrelated shapes: the visual counterpart of Webern's tone-color melodies. A Kandinsky abstract is like a set of Webernian wisps frozen onto canvas; Schoenberg sought out Kandinsky for lessons in painting.

By 1923, Schoenberg had brought his thoughts together for some kind of formulation. It was time, he said, for music to recognize that tonality had reached a dead end, that it was possible to exist atonally, without the classic centrality of a single key per musical composition. As a way of avoiding the creation of that centrality, Schoenberg proposed a complex mathematical principle by which a piece would be built out of the composer's ordering of all twelve chromatic tones—a "row" of tones so arranged that no one of them could be repeated until all twelve were heard in a complete series. The rules for "tone-row" or "serial" composition were strict only to the unimaginative; you only need hear the eloquence of some of the first generation of pure "row" compositions to judge the applicability in masterly hands.

Not long thereafter, the teacher and his disciples parted company. Schoenberg settled in Los Angeles, where he heard sporadic performances of his more difficult scores make little headway in the world. Berg died tragically young, his opera *Lulu*, a powerful work entirely based on a single twelve-tone row, incomplete. (It has recently been completed from the composer's fairly filled-out sketches.) Webern, who staunchly believed in Hitler's principles for saving the world, heard his music denounced on the Nazi-controlled radio as "cultural Bolshevism"; he was killed accidentally in the last days of the war, by a bullet from an occupying American soldier.

Yet, from these three innovators, promulgators of a new way of musical thinking (if not necessarily a brave new world), a powerful legacy exists. First, of course, there is the music: the soaring energy in Schoenberg's last quartets and in the speculative opera *Moses and Aaron* (for the completion of which he vainly, pathetically, begged for foundation support during his entire American sojourn). There is the haunting sadness in Berg's last complete work, the Violin Concerto, in which the twelve-tone writing is warm and laden with emotion, even before the row theme merges at the end with the melody of a Bach chorale. And there are the tiny wisps by Webern, exquisite and powerful works in which even the silences seem subjected to an artistic arrangement, that employ a serialism which goes philosophically beyond even Schoenberg's own principles.

SELECTED RECORDINGS

Schoenberg
Five Pieces for Orchestra
   –Günther Wand and the Gurzenich Orchestra of Cologne (with Webern's Cantata No. 1 and Stravinsky's *Dumbarton Oaks* Concerto) (Nonesuch)
Violin Concerto; Piano Concerto
   –Israel Baker, violinist, and Glenn Gould, pianist, respectively, with Robert Craft and the Columbia Symphony Orchestra (Columbia)

Berg
Three Pieces for Orchestra
   –Pierre Boulez and the BBC Symphony Orchestra (with Berg's Chamber Concerto) (Columbia)
Violin Concerto
   –Henryk Szeryng, violinist, with Rafael Kubelik and the Bavarian State Radio Orchestra (Deutsche Grammophon)

Webern
The complete music
   –various ensembles under the direction of Pierre Boulez (Columbia)

No conductor or soloist will attempt this music without a fair amount of conviction, public resistance (even to music dating as far back as 1908!) being what it is. Nonetheless, the pity is that the self-serving Robert Craft still accounts for the sole performances of much of this music. Fortunately, Craft's album of the entire output of Anton Webern (a lifetime on only four LPs) has been superseded by the spectacularly good set by Boulez, an album that should be the cornerstone of any collection showing an awareness of the music of this century.

The Boulez performance of Berg's pieces are also extraordinary; here is a real example of kindred spirits touching over a distance of one generation. Szeryng's performance of the Berg *Violin Concerto* meets the music with a finely controlled passion. This work, of course, is what you play for people who tell you that atonal music is devoid of emotion.

Arnold Schoenberg's 1936 violin concerto and the 1942 piano concerto are somewhat more forbidding than, say, the Berg score, and the two soloists' performances deserve better orchestral collaboration than Craft provides. Yet, both are monumental scores that grow to warmth on repeated hearings and Gould's performance, on its own, is an eloquent statement on Schoenberg's behalf.

Igor Stravinsky

b Oranienbaum (near St. Petersburg, Russia), June 17, 1882; *d* New York, April 6, 1971. Principal output includes: orchestral music (three symphonies plus the *Symphony of Psalms* for chorus and orchestra and the *Symphony of Winds*; concertos for violin and for piano with wind orchestra; other orchestral works called "concerto"; ballets for large and small orchestras; dances for Broadway theater and for the Ringling Bros. Circus); chamber music for almost all conceivable combinations (including voice); opera (the full-length *The Rake's Progress*, plus several shorter works); choral music both religious and secular (including a mass for chorus and winds); solo pieces; songs; reorchestrations of many works including "Happy Birthday"; and "The Star-Spangled Banner."

Stravinsky's career wonderfully demonstrates the old adage that greatness can often be the result of the right man in the right place at the right time. European music was, by 1900, virtually reeling under the weight of its own tradition; Gustav Mahler had made the question "what next?" virtually unanswerable. It took every ounce of energy by contemporary non-Germanic composers to resist the heady summons of Wagnerian and Mahlerian Romanticism.

Russian art, however, was still relatively new. Although Tchaikovsky can be thought to have wavered in the direction of the German influence, Russia's music still owed more to its own national roots than to outside forces. A new composer with a genuine overview could, therefore, profit much from outside influences without losing his native vigor. Such a composer Stravinsky proved to be.

His earliest scores had their roots partly in French tone painting and partly in the teachings of his own mentor, Rimsky-Korsakov. In his early 20s, Stravinsky attracted the attention of the legendary ballet impresario, Serge Diaghilev, who commissioned the scores that turned the world on its ear: *The Firebird*, *Petrouchka*, and, more than even these, *The Rite of Spring*, which, at its premiere on May 29, 1913, precipitated the kind of response that no press agent could have devised. The Parisians rioted, and Stravinsky's career was made.

But that famous riot was merely the last hurrah in the face of the inevitable. *The Rite*, with its use of the orchestra as no orchestra had been used before, its violent outbursts of raw, brutal energy, its strange and constantly shifting rhythms, was a billboard announcing that the old music was, indeed, dead and that the new music had begun. Stravinsky never repeated the manner of *The Rite*; either his own instincts or the nihilism bred out of the First World War or a combination brought him to yet another style, an evocation of the old classicism in music of an almost dry, glinty clarity. Yet the old Stravinsky showed his shadow. The first of these "neo-classic" pieces, *The Soldier's Tale* of 1918 for speakers and small orchestra, or *The Wedding* of 1920 for chorus and percussion ensemble, were still overlain with the spirit of Russian folksong as the early ballets had been. It is likely, therefore, that the new classicism was, for Stravinsky, a refinement of the essential personality that was always there.

To discuss Stravinsky's career is, in fact, to discuss virtually all important currents in 20th-century music. In the 1930s, first in Paris and later ensconced as Hollywood's *grand seigneur* of serious music, he continued to rework classic formulas, dabbled in American commercial jazz (*Ebony Concerto*, written in 1946 for the Woody Herman orchestra), wrote a Broadway ballet (*Scènes de Ballet*, for a Billy Rose extravaganza) and *Polka (1942) for Circus Elephants*, as well as extended symphonies and concertos. In 1951, he startled the world with his opera *The Rake's Progress*, almost a paraphrase of Italian bel-canto opera of a century before, and startled the world again immediately thereafter by appearing to adopt the atonal musical style of his long-presumed mortal rival (and fellow Hollywood *grand seigneur*) Arnold Schoenberg. Even here, however, the atonal works of Stravinsky are full of his own individuality, the mature expressive dignity that he had always possessed.

That is, perhaps, the keynote of Stravinsky's genius—that, in an increasingly accelerated world, Stravinsky was able to embrace the multifarious changes in the complexion of music while remaining constant to an inner voice. "I don't change," he once said. "I just add."

SELECTED RECORDINGS

The Firebird (complete ballet); **Petrouchka** (complete ballet); **The Rite of Spring**
  –Igor Stravinsky and the Columbia Symphony Orchestra (three separate disks) (Columbia/CBS)
The Rite of Spring
  –Pierre Boulez and the Cleveland Orchestra (Columbia/CBS)
Four Ballets: *Apollo Musagetes, Orpheus, Pulcinella, Le Baiser de la Fée*
  –Igor Stravinsky and the Columbia Symphony Orchestra (three-record album) (Columbia/CBS)
Symphony in C; Symphony of Psalms
  –Igor Stravinsky and the Canadian Broadcasting Symphony (with chorus in the *Symphony of Psalms*) (Columbia/CBS)
Symphony in Three Movements; Violin Concerto in D
  –Igor Stravinsky and the Columbia Symphony (with Isaac Stern, soloist, in the Violin Concerto) (Columbia)

"The New Stravinsky" (single record of short works, including *Abraham and Isaac*, *Introitus*, *T. S. Eliot in Memoriam*, *The Requiem Canticles*, and Variations for Orchestra);
   —various soloists, the Ithaca College Chorus, with Igor Stravinsky and Robert Craft and the Columbia Symphony Orchestra (Columbia)

A choice of performances in Stravinsky's case is relatively easy, as nearly all of his major scores are available in recordings conducted either by him or by his protégé, Robert Craft. And, while it does not always follow that composers (or their protégés) are automatically the best interpreters of their music, both Stravinsky and Craft are reasonably acceptable exceptions. The works in the above list give a fairly complete picture of Stravinsky's style, from the early ballets of Russian inspiration (which make sense only when heard in their complete version rather than in the "suites" of excerpts arranged by Stravinsky and others) to the stupendous *Rite of Spring*, to the neo-classic ballets of the 1920s and 1930s (including the *Pulcinella*, which is actually a free paraphrase of music by the Italian Baroque composer Giovanni Pergolesi, and *Le Baiser de la Fée*, which imaginatively subjects music by Tchaikovsky to the same treatment). The two symphonies are marvelous works, both somewhat classic in their outline; yet the Symphony in Three Movements does return at times to the dazzling rhythms of *The Rite of Spring*. "The New Stravinsky" is a good representation of the composer's last decade, when he placed his own personal seal on the same atonality of Schoenberg and his disciples, which he had previously proclaimed himself at odds.

There are, of course, many approaches to Stravinsky's music, performances by several conductors (including, notably, Colin Davis, Leonard Bernstein, and, for the early ballets, Carlo Maria Giulini) that are somewhat more warm-blooded than the meticulous, sharp-edged playing preferred by Stravinsky himself. The Boulez performance of *The Rite of Spring* is many degrees warmer than the composer's own, although Stravinsky is said to have detested it. A work of this stature can be approached in many ways.

Béla Bartók

b Nagy Szent Miklos, Transylvania, March 25, 1881; *d* New York, September 26, 1945. Principal output includes: orchestral works (three piano concertos, two violin concertos, *Concerto for Orchestra*, *Music for Strings, Percussion and Celesta*, two ballets, Dance Suite, Divertimento for String Orchestra); chamber music (six string quartets, numerous works for other combinations); piano music (including *Mikrokosmos*, six books of teaching pieces of graduated difficulty); the opera *Duke Bluebeard's Castle*; and choral and vocal music, much of which paraphrases Magyar and Balkan folk music.

Like his near-contemporary Stravinsky, Bartók's first obsession was to bring the spirit of his own country's folk music into a larger context; to this end, he spent years in the field, recording and notating the exact nature of Eastern European songs and dances. His great skill at assimilating the essence of this music gives his own works much of their fascinating rhythmic flexibility and their pounding, often percussive rhythms. Like Stravinsky, too, Bartók could use an entire string section, a piano or two—almost any instrumental force, however unlikely—as a vast percussion device. In doing so, he also accomplished the reverse; Bartók's percussiveness has its own strange, haunting melodic power.

His early music—the ballet *The Wooden Prince*, in particular—was somewhat under the Impressionist influence, with even a trace of Liszt. But Bartók was quick to find his voice. A shy man, he was seldom honored as he merited, in his native Hungary or in the United States when he settled there in the mid-1930s. (His first teaching job in New York was not as composer, but as a scholar in ethnic music!) His edgy, thrillingly vital music, with its spooky evocations of night sounds (as in the slow movement of the *Music for*

Strings, Percussion and Celesta and in several of the string quartets), won devotees only slowly. His countryman, the great violinist Joseph Szigeti, played his music and pleaded his cause; even Benny Goodman commissioned him to do a work for Goodman, Szigeti, and Bartók to play (*Contrasts*). To no avail; Bartók died in poverty, with the knowledge that he still had a great deal of music to compose.

In his last year he did enjoy something like acclaim. Two works—the Third Piano Concerto (again with its gorgeous section of night sounds) and the fabulously inventive Concerto for Orchestra—won great acclaim from press and public. They were, to be sure, somewhat more "accessible" than his acerbic earlier scores; it was not that Bartók had decided to write for quick success, but that, like Brahms in his last chamber music and Wagner in his *Parsifal*, he had found the gift to be both spiritual and simple. By the time the acclaim from these works had caught up with him, however, Béla Bartók was dead.

SELECTED RECORDINGS

Concerto for Orchestra
   –Fritz Reiner and the Chicago Symphony Orchestra (RCA)
Piano Concertos Nos. 1–3
   –Stephen Bishop-Kovacevitch, soloist, with Colin Davis and the London Symphony or BBC Symphony Orchestra (Philips)
Piano Concertos Nos. 2 & 3
   –Geza Anda, soloist, with Ferenc Fricsay and the Berlin Radio Symphony Orchestra (Deutsche Grammophon)
Music for Strings, Percussion and Celesta
   –Fritz Reiner and the Chicago Symphony Orchestra (RCA)
Violin Concerto No.2 in B minor
   –Henryk Szeryng, soloist, with Bernard Haitink and the Amsterdam Concertgebouw Orchestra (Philips)

It does not always follow that a composer's compatriots are his best interpreters; indeed, the Bartók performances by the Hungarian Antal Dorati are distinctly poor. Fritz Reiner, whether because of his Hungarian blood or simply his superb command of his craft, always conducted Bartók's music stunningly, and the virtuosity of the Chicago Symphony in its Reiner days is perfectly suited to the fantasy and energy in the concerto and the *Music*. Anda's superlative performances of the piano concertos are challenged by the complete set by the young American (of Slavic descent) Stephen Bishop-Kovacevitch (with the very non-Slavic Colin Davis providing splendid support); you win either way.

The 1938 Violin Concerto is another work teeming with energy; its "empty" opening (mere chords "strummed" by the orchestra) is probably a humorous touch, an infinitesimal musical acorn giving rise to a mighty forest. Again, as so often, Szeryng is best attuned to the music's many kinds of drama.

TWO
SOVIET COMPOSERS

Sergei Prokofiev
b Ekaterinoslav, April 23, 1891;
d Moscow, March 4, 1953

Dmitri Shostakovich
b St. Petersburg, September 25, 1906;
d Moscow, August 9, 1975

Principal output includes: orchestral music (Prokofiev: seven symphonies, five piano concertos, two violin concertos, and one cello concerto rewritten as a *Sinfonia Concertante* for cello and orchestra; Shostakovich: fifteen symphonies, two piano concertos, two violin concertos, and two cello concertos); by both composers: vast quantities of music for ballet, film, and incidental occasions; several operas, cantatas, and other choral pieces; chamber music, including string quartets; and vast amounts of piano music and songs.

Sergei Prokofiev

While Soviet Russia consolidated itself as a world power after the Revolution, Prokofiev—already a composer of considerable renown—was becoming the daring young man of music in the West: in the United States, where he introduced his first three piano concertos and wrote the satiric opera *The Love of Three Oranges*, and in Paris. Fifteen years younger, Dmitri Shostakovich was developing his musical style under Russian guidance at home. By the time Prokofiev finally returned to Russia, in 1933, Shostakovich had already attracted attention with a successful symphony, the comic opera *The Nose*, and a growing output in all musical forms.

Both composers languished under Stalinist musical edicts; it is tantalizing but fruitless to speculate on what either would have accomplished in the so-called "free world" (which means, in music, that artists are free to go broke, without the state subsidy guaranteed their oppressed Soviet brethren, when they behave). It

Dmitri Shostakovich

is obvious that the vivacious sense of *grotesquerie* demonstrated by Shostakovich in his First Symphony and the *Age of Gold* ballet (1924 and 1929, respectively) was much diluted in his later works, where it becomes a sort of nose-thumbing at familiar music of the West. It is equally obvious that Prokofiev's early mastery of a brilliant, dissonant musical style, as in the Third Piano Concerto of 1921 and even earlier in the *Scythian Suite* of 1914, gave way in his Soviet music to the robust romanticism of the *Romeo and Juliet* ballet of 1935 and the Fifth Symphony of 1944.

Yet these are outstanding masterpieces, enough to earn Prokofiev's fame as a great composer in a carefully modulated post-Romantic style. And the later works of Shostakovich, while giving way to a kind of diffuseness and an oppressive vulgarity, include such strong pieces as the Fifth Symphony, with its genial blend of Mahler and Tchaikovsky, and the marvelous, lighthearted Ninth, almost Mozartian in its simplicity. Late in his life, for reasons of conscience poignantly revealed in memoirs smuggled out of the Soviet Union after his death, Shostakovich found a way to inject a tone of personality, even of torment, into his music without alienating the authorities. Symphonies Nos. 13 and 14, with their settings of poetry that cry out loudly against social injustice, have a style that is, for Shostakovich, spare, terse, and immensely expressive.

SELECTED RECORDINGS

Prokofiev
Classical Symphony in D major; Symphony No. 7
  —Gennadi Rozhdestvensky and the Moscow State Radio Orchestra (Angel)
Symphony No. 5 in B-flat major
  —Leonard Bernstein and the New York Philharmonic Orchestra (Columbia)
Five Piano Concertos
  —Vladimir Ashkenazy, pianist, with Andre Previn and the London Symphony Orchestra (three-record album; records available separately) (London/Decca)
Violin Concertos Nos. 1 and 2
  —Isaac Stern, violinist, with Eugene Ormandy and the Philadelphia Orchestra (Columbia)
Romeo and Juliet (complete ballet)
  —Lorin Maazel and the Cleveland Orchestra (London/Decca)

Shostakovich
Symphonies Nos. 1 and 9
  —Leonard Bernstein and the New York Philharmonic Orchestra (Columbia)
Symphony No. 5
  —Maxim Shostakovich and the USSR Symphony Orchestra (Angel/HMV)
Symphony No. 14
  —Galina Vishnevskaya, soprano, with Mstislav

Rostropovitch and the Moscow Philharmonic
Orchestra (Columbia/HMV)
Symphony No. 15
  –Maxim Shostakovich and the Moscow Radio
  Symphony Orchestra (Angel/HMV)

From the early *Classical* Symphony, with its genial
spoof of genuine classicism, to the tepid romanticism
of the doctrinaire Seventh, Prokofiev's last symphony,
is a sad study in decline of a creative spirit not its own
master. The superior Fifth Symphony, with its haunting, almost Mozartian line in the slow movement, is a
way station in this decline; here at least Prokofiev
could manage a conservative mode of expression without compromise. Yet, there is so much vitality in the
five piano concertos—most of all, in the glistening
Second and Third—and in the demoniac solo writing
in the two violin concertos, that one must regret the
fetters that Prokofiev was obliged to accept, probably
as penance for his long absence from his native soil.

The cheeky Shostakovich First Symphony was,
similarly, the work of a 19-year-old iconoclast with
limitless horizons; yet, he seldom if ever touched that
vein again. The Fifth, Shostakovich's most popular
symphony, does generate a fine, brave power, and the
performance under Shostakovich's talented son, Maxim, gives the work a greater eloquence than most
American versions possess. The somber No. 14 and the
lovely, featherbrained No. 15 show a late mastery over
concise expression.

The Russian orchestras are often wobbly, but the
tone of the playing is authentic and powerful. On the
other hand, the team of Stern and Ormandy has the
ideal romantic spirit for the two early Prokofiev violin
concertos, and Ashkenazy conquers the minefields in
the piano concertos with outrageous ease. More than
anything else by either composer, Prokofiev's *Romeo
and Juliet* will haunt you after one hearing, and anything less than a complete recording (like the one performed with splendid fervor under Maazel) is a
deprivation not to be endured.

IVES
AND THE AMERICANS

Charles Ives

b Danbury, Connecticut, October 20, 1874; *d* New
York City, May 19, 1954. Principal output includes:
orchestral music (four symphonies, plus the
Holidays Symphony; suites of descriptive music—
Three Places in New England, for example—and
several short characteristic pieces); chamber music,
including two quartets; the cantata *The Celestial
Country*; piano pieces, songs; and a fair amount of
music not easy to classify.

In the 1930s, the American
critic Paul Rosenfeld called
Charles Ives "the foremost of
the Americans who have expressed their feelings of life
in musical forms." Since Rosenfeld's time, American musical language has developed
a world-recognized originality, yet nothing has happened
since his evaluation of Ives to
alter his view. If anything,
Ives's reputation and influ-
ence are still on the ascendant; his Third and Fourth
symphonies, the *Three Places in New England*, and the
Concord sonata (for piano) are the works most likely to
be held at the present time as representative of greatness in American music.

The wonder is, therefore, that Ives wrote most of
his compositions before the end of the First World
War. For the rest of the time (being independently
well-off as an insurance broker) he sat back and
grumped, waiting for the world to catch up to his
iconoclastic musical ideas, concocting outrageous, ill-
tempered rationalizations for why it took the world so
long. Success and recognition finally came. In 1947 his

Third Symphony won the Pulitzer Prize—thirty-six years after it was composed!

Emerging at a time when American music, such as it was, was largely the creation of composers trained in the conservatories of Europe, Ives devoted himself furiously to a ransacking of native musical resources to develop a truly American style. In all but results, therefore, he resembles an American Dvořák, say, or Mussorgsky; yet, his style at the turn of the century strangely prefigured advanced musical experiments that would be performed in Europe decades later: two keys, or two rhythms, heard simultaneously, that sort of thing. There may be some reason to suspect Ives of hitting upon his "modernisms" out of sheer Yankee cussedness rather than deep conviction. That in no way affects the raw, rugged power of his music.

By the time Ives's music was dusted off and found important—from 1947 on—American music had generally advanced a great distance from where Ives had found it. And yet the first generations of Americans went about establishing a national style in exactly the way Ives had: through seeking out indigenous music and incorporating it into larger forms. Thus spake George Gershwin (1898–1937) in the symphonic works inspired by his own solid grounding in the early forms of jazz; thus, Aaron Copland (1900–) in the 1930s and 1940s in such works as the ballets *Rodeo* and *Billy the Kid*; thus, Roy Harris (1898–1979) in his Third Symphony with its folk elements lurking behind grinding dissonances; thus, Virgil Thomson (1896–) in his film scores and operas full of folk and hymn tunes.

The Second World War and its preceding years had sent to America some of the major European figures: Schoenberg, Stravinsky, Bartók, and others. Most of them made themselves available to a new generation of Americans who were to become the next composers. From the war's end onward, the easy Americanisms of the earlier years were put aside, or at least somewhat subtilized. Men like Roger Sessions (1896–) and Elliott Carter (1908–) came to the fore, their music reaching out to claim a place in the international mainstream, strongly dissonant, brilliant in its mastery of orchestral effect and of rhythm, and no longer condescending in order to win easy approval with cowboy tunes and the like. (Copland, too, partook of America's musical growth, with such large-scale and uncompromising later scores as the Third Symphony of 1946.)

A dichotomy soon grew between the conservatives here and the progressives there; by the mid-1950s, the output of new music in America could include such things as a work by Gunther Schuller (1925–), involving an amalgamation of twelve-tone writing and contemporary jazz; something of pure neo-Romanticism by, say, John La Montaine (1920–) or Alan Hovhaness (1911–); or something wildly experimental for flutes and ashcans. A rash of fervent creativity swept America, impelled by a national pride that the music by the country's major composers was no longer heard as something quaint from the New World, but as a major contribution to the musical mainstream, which stood or fell on its quality. Charles Ives saw the beginnings, and died proud.

SELECTED RECORDINGS

Ives
**Symphony No. 3; Central Park in the Dark;
Decoration Day; The Unanswered Question**
 –Leonard Bernstein and the New York
 Philharmonic (Columbia)
Symphony No. 4
 –Seiji Ozawa and the Boston Symphony Orchestra
 (Deutsche Grammophon)
Three Places in New England
 –Michael Tilson Thomas and the Boston
 Symphony Orchestra (Deutsche Grammophon)

Harris
Symphony No. 3 (with Bernstein's *Jeremiah*
symphony)
 –Leonard Bernstein and the New York
 Philharmonic (Columbia/CBS)

Copland
**Rodeo; Appalachian Spring; Billy the Kid;
El Salón México**
 –Leonard Bernstein and the New York
 Philharmonic (two records) (Columbia)

Symphony No. 3
–Leonard Bernstein and the New York
Philharmonic (Columbia/CBS)

Carter
Concerto for Orchestra (with William Schuman, *In
Praise of Shahn*)
–Leonard Bernstein and the New York
Philharmonic (Columbia)
Double Concerto; Variations for Orchestra
–Frederick Prausnitz and the New Philharmonia
Orchestra (Columbia)

Sessions
Rhapsody for Orchestra; Symphony No. 8
–Frederick Prausnitz and the New Philharmonia
Orchestra (Argo)

Imbrie
Violin Concerto
–Carol Glenn, violinist, with Zoltan Rozsnyai and
the Columbia Symphony Orchestra (Columbia
Special Products)

The above listing is merely a sampling of American
creativity from Ives to the near-past—from 1903, the
year of *Three Places in New England*, to 1970, the year of
the Carter *Concerto for Orchestra*, the Sessions *Rhapsody*,
and William Schuman's *In Praise of Shahn*. That similar-
ities in style—in the handling of dissonance, and in
pure gumption—exist among these earliest and latest
works is, of course, testimony most of all to the prophetic nature of Charles Ives.

Like the Copland ballets, the Harris Third Symphony has a comfortable datedness about it; that is not
Harris's fault, but merely the fact that composers for
Western motion pictures and television series have
picked the style dry. Yet, as with *Hamlet*, the clichés
are freshest the first time around. The power of the
later Copland, especially the dazzling display of pure
motor energy that ends the Third Symphony, more
than atones for the easy early music.

Sessions, and his brilliant former pupil Andrew
Imbrie, carry much of the intellectual weight of
American musical expression; yet it is remarkable how
the elder Sessions, in the two works listed here, refines

his style and reveals its emotional impact. The Imbrie concerto dates from 1958; it remains one of the most original and powerful American scores, and its current neglect in America and elsewhere is unpardonable.

It goes without saying that the performances here listed, most of them unduplicated anyhow, are authoritative. Nobody performs such difficult music if he doesn't know how.

SUPPLEMENTARY COMPOSERS

Paul Hindemith (1895–1963)
Kammermusik Nos. 5 and 6
–Concerto Amsterdam (Telefunken)
Mathis der Maler (Symphony)
–Eugene Ormandy and the Philadelphia Orchestra (Columbia/CBS)

Kurt Weill (1900–1950)
Symphonies Nos. 1 (1921) **and 2** (1933)
–Gary Bertini and the BBC Symphony Orchestra (Argo)

Manuel de Falla (1876–1946)
The Three-cornered Hat (complete ballet);
Harpsichord Concerto
–Jan DeGaetani, soprano, Igor Kipnis, harpsichordist, and Pierre Boulez and the New York Philharmonic (Columbia)

Sir William Walton (1902–)
Suites from the film scores to Henry V and Richard III
–Sir William Walton and the Philharmonia Orchestra (Seraphim/HMV)

Carl Nielsen (1865–1931)
Symphony No. 5
–Leonard Bernstein and the New York Philharmonic (Columbia)

Only with historical hindsight will we be able to fill in completely the stylistic image of 20th-century music. Yet, here are a few more landmarks to suggest further exploration on your own. Hindemith, who was born and died in Germany but taught in the United States for many years, was a curiously individualistic composer; active while Schoenberg was formulating his twelve-tone theories, Hindemith stood apart, working with a lean, ascetic style bristling with counterpoint but never divorced from a feeling of tonality. His *Chamber Music* pieces (actually for small orchestra) have a marvelous drive and a sense of constant adventure; they have been likened to the "Brandenburg" Concertos of Bach. Later—in the late 1930s, say—Hindemith's style became warmer. Both Brahms and Bach are echoed in his philosophical opera about Mathias Grünewald, the mystical German painter, from which he later drew a "symphony" of three descriptive pieces. The result, known as *Mathis der Maler*, remains his most popular piece.

The younger Kurt Weill was also active in Berlin during the time when Schoenberg cast his shadow. Though known today mostly for his marvelously strong theater music, written in collaboration with Bertolt Brecht and others, Weill had previously had a career as a serious composer, and the First Symphony, only recently rediscovered, is full of a gleaming, diabolical strength. The Second Symphony, written just as Weill and his wife were fleeing Hitler's Germany, is an even stronger piece, echoing some of the powerful theater music, but developing its own terrific energy.

The remaining three composers are major figures in countries that were outside what we usually regard as the musical mainstream. England's William Walton was (and is) prolific in many media, but his splendid film music represents the high level that this genre seldom reaches. Falla was the most original composer to work in Spain; his brief, intense Harpsichord Concerto has some of the mystery of late paintings by El Greco, while the comic ballet is the most artful blending of Spanish rhythms and original dramatic writing. Denmark's Carl Nielsen wrote six symphonies that have only recently made their way into the world's repertoire, thanks largely to the advocacy of Leonard Bernstein. They are extraordinarily powerful works, somewhat reminiscent of Mahler, but full of a raucous wit in one movement and a profound spirituality in the next that together set Nielsen in a class by himself.

AFTERWORD

Everybody agrees that the art of music is at a crossroads, but everyone has always agreed on that point at any time in history. Yet, as suggested a few pages back, the crisis in orchestral music is very real: the parting of the ways between those who would advance the musical language into unknown regions and those who, in return for paying the bills for culture, feel that they have the right to be entertained with a minimum of thinking.

Was it ever thus? No, not always. Johannes Brahms stood with tears in his eyes, the most modern composer in Vienna at the time, receiving the crowd's acclaim for his newest music. But analogies with the past are hard to support.

They are, most of all, because technology has come to play so crucial a part in the musical life of all of us. The incredible facilities for the recording and transmission of information have had, as one effect, a drastic speedup of the rate of artistic change. Whereas a Brahms, say, or even a Beethoven, worked in a style that had had some validity for a matter of decades, pushing back the horizons just a little more with every new composition, today's composer works against a crazed acceleration of rate of change. A style may be in vogue one week, heard immediately and imitated all over the world thanks to records and broadcasts, and a week later the style has been exhausted.

Has music become its own worst enemy? Not really; it has raced ahead of the normal process of assimilation and understanding, but sooner or later the world catches up. And change has a surprising knack, now and then, of racing backwards, too—or, as a philosopher put it more elegantly, progress consists of three steps forward and two backward. At the start of the 1980s, for example, there is the usual fear-racked talk of iconoclasm and innovation; yet some composers seem to have rediscovered the ideals of tonality and are writing new works in this style.

But genuine experiments continue. A style known as "minimalism" (a term borrowed from painting), consisting of tiny musical patterns repeated at great length and oozing into new patterns ever so slowly, has produced some works of extreme popularity from composers Steve Reich and Philip Glass. An entire work—well, call it opera for lack of a proper new word—by Philip Glass and the American playwright Robert Wilson, called *Einstein on the Beach* and lasting some four hours uninterrupted, was a sensational success in New York and Paris in the 1976–77 music season; does the musical future lie here?

Meanwhile, the notion of deriving musical patterns from electronic sources, developed in German radio studios in the 1950s, continues to engage some of the brightest musical minds today. New technology involving computers gives composers an infinitely greater personal control over the nature and design of their electronic works than had been possible in the early days, and thrilling music is coming out of, to cite two sources, the computer-music laboratories at Stanford University in California and at the IRCAM studios maintained by Pierre Boulez in Paris. Does the musical future lie here? At least there's a possible repertoire here that doesn't need the symphony orchestra for its realization.

Leonard Bernstein, one of the most dynamic conductors of his day, pronounced in the late 1960s that the symphony orchestra as an institution was already dead. Ten years later, Bernstein was still writing music for the symphony orchestra—and hearing it performed. Critics proclaimed that Beethoven was bringing the art of music to a debauched end; another generation proclaimed it of Wagner; another screamed blue murder at the premiere of Stravinsky's *The Rite of Spring*, that was in 1913. Stravinsky himself was to compose for symphony orchestra for another half-century; and so did many others. And they still do.

PICTURE CREDITS

The main text of this book is set in Compano Roman; the headings in Goudy.
Printed on 70 pound Finch Opaque, Vellum.